The Blessed Woman
A Devotional Study of the Sermon on the Mount

Pam Jenkins

PublishAmerica
Baltimore

© 2008 by Pam Jenkins.
All rights reserved. No part of this book may be reproduced, stored in a retrieval system or transmitted in any form or by any means without the prior written permission of the publishers, except by a reviewer who may quote brief passages in a review to be printed in a newspaper, magazine or journal.

First printing

PublishAmerica has allowed this work to remain exactly as the author intended, verbatim, without editorial input.

"Scripture taken from the New American Standard Bible®, Copyright © 1960,1962,1963,1968,1971,1972,1973,1975,1977,1995 by The Lockman Foundation. Used by permission." (www.Lockman.org) Scriptures quotations identified KJV are from the King James Version.

ISBN: 1-60474-105-8
PUBLISHED BY PUBLISHAMERICA, LLLP
www.publishamerica.com
Baltimore

Printed in the United States of America

To Granny,

*Who inspired me to live for something greater than myself.
Who's heart belonged to her God.*

Foreword

   Have you ever asked yourself the question: "How did I get to this place in my life?" Or even the most powerful two worded question there is: "What happened"? We all have those moments when we look up in total amazement scratching our heads trying to figure out how our lives ended up on the course that led us to the place we find ourselves in. We wonder what went wrong or even what went right? We are all on a path beloved. But what path are you on or from what path have you strayed? Is it the uncertainty of your future that has taken you off the beaten path or is it your past that has led you back to the path you once trod? Every step you have taken thus far whether by free will or by events beyond your control, have led you to the place where you are. Steps all moving together to tell a story…your story. Each footprint writing its own line, and filling its own page with the days of your life.
   There are many footprints… many stories being masterfully written all under the watchful eye of a Sovereign God. People have a secret history with God. Pages never intended to be read by anyone else. Parts of the stories that we may never be privy to because it was so sacred between God and His child. It's these hidden story lines of people's lives that if we could take that rare glimpse, would read them with fear and trembling. It's in these sacred lines that the struggles and heartaches are penned. The intimate details of the lives of people as they journeyed with God along the path. We may see them on the mountaintop but we do not know of the climb to the top or of the descent into the valley below. We may hear the Victory cry but we never hear the sounds

of the marching through the battlefield. We may witness the life that resounds His praise but never know of the tears they shed through heartache. Secret pages held by God, drawn up close to His heart and kept there until the day your story is told. The story that tells of the blessed life.

The blessed life is not found upon the mountains but is discovered in the deep valleys below. It is hidden in the rubble like a precious treasure buried in the ashes, tucked away like a rare jewel, cloaked in the veil of suffering. The blessed life is that refreshing spring that is unearthed only in the well of tears…the silver vessel that is molded in the ambers of the fiery furnace, a sweet aroma released in the crushing of a delicate rose.

We want a blessed life, a happy life but without changing our lifestyle. We want a quick fix to our situations, an "easy" button. If just the right button, the right church, the right counselor, relationship, etc… or when the cure all doesn't happen in one fell swoop, the result is guilt, depression, an overwhelming sense of hopelessness, and failure. The questions that haunt the soul that has lost hope is: *"What's wrong with me? Is there real happiness? Will I ever find it?"* Ironically, looking for an experience that will set us free often times puts us in bondage. We are the keepers of our prisons.

Charles Wesley once said: *"He speaks, and listening to his voice new life the dead receive, the mournful, broken hearts rejoice, the humble poor believe."* If you could take your fingers and take hold of the hand of God, there clasped tightly in the palm of Sovereignty you would find every day of your life laid out in perfect order. The perfect number of days, hours and minutes etched out with skill and perfection, woven into the very fabric of the will of the Almighty. God, the Master Artist, purposefully painted every detail of every day of your life for they were created in the depths of eternity by the Eternal One Himself before you were ever born. There is nothing that will happen in your life that could ever take Him by surprise for He Himself has seen it, He has ordained it and established it in His loving providence. Before He formed your feet of clay He had already carved out the path that they were to walk upon.

When you awoke this morning your Heavenly Father was seated on His throne reigning over the entire universe and so it will be when you lay your head down to rest this evening. For He is ever seated with all power and authority on the very throne of grace. It is here in this seat of sovereignty that He has been every day, every moment of your life, lovingly watching over every detail.

God has not planned a work in your life, you are His work, and you are His life, His wonderful masterpiece. He has been with you since the moment you took your first breath for He breathed life into you and He will be with you when you breathe your last for He is your future. You are His namesake and He is your God. He is your Father and you are His child. He has a plan for your life beloved woman. A master plan for a blessed life.

As you hold this book, know that it is God who has ordained this moment in your life for you to hold these pages in your hands. It is His hands that brought you to this place, this moment in time to set you on a journey to a place in order to sit you at the feet of His only begotten Son, Jesus Christ. He wants us to have and know what it means to have a blessed life according to His perfect design. Over two thousand years ago, Jesus looked out into the faces of a multitude of listeners and shared with them the secrets of the blessed life. But were His words easy? Did He paint such a grand picture of the blessed life that it would be sought after by millions? Is Jesus' description of a blessed life appealing at first glance? Does the blessed life mean no worries, no sickness, no suffering, no poverty or pain? Does it mean that our bank accounts will be big and our troubles small? How does Jesus intend for us to live while we are on this earth? How are we to spend our days?

Jesus said: "I am the way, the truth and the life". If He is the life then the only way we can have real life, or the blessed life is according to His truth, His way. His life cannot be found apart from His truth or apart from His way. We will take that journey to the Sermon on the Mount and listen to truth Himself and in the listening we will find the way, the only way to the blessed life that so many are in search of. But it is only found here in this one place…Jesus.

Pre-Journey Assignment

Your pre-journey assignment should be done before you begin your study. These are always thought provoking but they are also intended to bring out what's in our heart and in our mind. It's intended to reveal our way of thinking, our ideologies and bring insight into why our very lifestyle is the way it is. I want to encourage you to give your pre-journey assignment time and for you to answer each question as detailed as possible. If you should require more space than has been allowed for your answers then use a separate sheet of paper. This assignment will always be a private one between you and the Lord. Ask Him to help you see yourself as you really are.

It's hard to put an exact definition on happiness isn't it? Have you ever met someone that just seemed to be happy all the time? I have. I'll never forget our Fed-ex deliveryman. He was a short little fellow and he seemed to have a skip in his step as he walked through our office doors just about on a daily basis. He was always whistling and always smiling. In the many years that he came through our office I never once saw him without a smile splashed across his face. He was truly a happy soul and a delight to everyone in the office that encountered him. In fact he had a phrase that he used when someone asked him, "How are you today?" His reply was always the same as he sported a big smile saying; "If I were any better, I'd have to be twins!" I always loved that. I would ask him how he was doing just to hear him say it. In fact I've adopted that phrase myself. Joy is absolutely contagious when it is genuine and it always leaves the one who has encountered it asking the question: "I wonder why that person is so happy?"

I want us to walk through this pre-journey assignment together as we think about true happiness. You may need some time to really think on these questions. You never want to rush a pre-journey assignment for they are always critical to our studies.

Would you consider yourself to be a happy person?

No - Not really

If you answered yes, then write out why you are a happy person. What makes you happy? What are the things in your life that bring you happiness?

If you answered no, then write out what it would take to make you happy? Have you ever thought about why you are unhappy?

To be content in my own skin, to know that I have a purpose and I am walking in that purpose

Do you believe that God wants for us to be happy?

_No_

Explain why or why not?

Happiness changes with conditions. I think God wants us to be holy.

Do you believe it's possible for someone to be truly happy no matter what his or her circumstances are? Explain your answer.

No, I believe that would be the definition of joy

What do you want to do with the life that God has given to you? How do you want to spend the rest of your days from this point forward?

living on purpose

THE BLESSED WOMAN

_____

_____

_____

Are you satisfied how you've spent your life thus far? What would you change or not change about it? What regrets do you have if any?

No, I have made some major mistakes that have affected not only myself but my son as well. I don't regret b/c God has used everything in my life for His glory

I understand you may be saying, "Pam, these are difficult questions." These are difficult questions beloved because they make us look back and they cause us to look forward! Surveying our lives is necessary for a bright future and looking ahead is vital to accepting our past. God has written a story just for you precious student. We just have to learn to follow the story line.

That's all beloved student. I will see you on day one of our study. Much love to you!

Lesson One
Who Will Enter the Kingdom of Heaven?

Day One

    Jesus had been traveling throughout all of Galilee teaching and proclaiming the Gospel of the Kingdom to all who would listen, healing every kind of disease and sickness among the people. The news about Jesus spread rapidly and because of this there were throngs of people flocking to Him for healing, comfort from pain and freedom from demons. Can you imagine, even for a moment, what it must have been like to be a spectator in the crowd when Jesus was present? How powerful it must have been to see blinded eyes open for the first time or to witness a leper's spots disappear at just a touch from the hand of Jesus. What excitement must have filled the air as Jesus made His way through the crowd. In the midst of all this popularity, Jesus retreats to a hillside side to share the most powerful words that His disciples would ever hear. Why would Jesus choose this moment to leave the throngs of people who were in desperate need, to speak on a more personal level with His followers? Why would He cease from doing such miraculous workings to sit down and share the message that He did? What could possibly be more important than healing someone who was sick, or delivering someone who was under demonic oppression? Yet, in the midst of great need, Jesus retreats and sits down to teach the words that we have come to know as the Sermon on the Mount. Could these words that Jesus spoke on this hillside be more important than healings, more important than deliverance from bondage, more important than seeing or hearing for the first time? It is at the asking of these questions that we begin our study on the blessed life. For this is why Jesus stopped everything He was doing to speak these powerful words on the blessed life.

Let's begin by going to the Lord, asking Him to give us ears to listen and a heart to understand His Words to us. Once you've finished, I'll meet you back here.

Now that you've finished praying, I want you to turn to the back of this study and there you will find Matthew chapters 5, 6 and 7 typed out for you. These chapters will be our main text of study and by the time we are finished these verses will be as a familiar friend to your heart. Take time now and read through these three chapters. It's always best to read through a passage of study non-stop the first time or two before you begin looking at it more thoroughly.

Write out in your own words what you think the purpose of Jesus' message was. I know this is a broad question because Jesus covers a lot of things in these three chapters, but just take a few moments to think about it and re-read through the text again if you need to before answering. Remember, there is no wrong or right answer.

The purpose of Jesus teaching the Sermon on the mount is to tell the blessings of what is in store for Gods children and responsibility we have in keeping his word.

Take a blue colored pencil and read through the text once more. As you do this, draw a rectangle around every reference to the Kingdom of Heaven. Sometimes you will see the phrase *"kingdom of heaven"* and other times you will see just the word *heaven* or *kingdom.* Make sure you mark all of these for they all pertain to the Kingdom of Heaven in these chapters.

Once you've finished marking these places, go back and review each one. Make a list of everything you learned about the Kingdom of Heaven in the space provided for you.

Kingdom of Heaven

According to these chapters, who will inherit the Kingdom of Heaven? I'll give you a hint: there are four of them—three of them are found in chapter five and one in chapter seven. These should be easy to locate because you've already marked the text for Kingdom of Heaven. See if you can find these! As you list them, write the scripture reference next to each one so you won't forget where you found them.

- *Blessed are the poor in spirit (Matt 5:3)*
- *Blessed are those who are persecuted for righteous sake (5:10)*
- *Whoever practice and teaches these commands (5:19)*
- *Only the one who does the will of my Father will inherit... (Matt 7:20)*

Did you find all four? These are powerful truths about those who will enter the Kingdom of Heaven. Through our study together this week we will look at each of these individually. Just from the list you made, in your own words write out a brief description of the person who will enter the Kingdom of Heaven. Remember, we are making this list from what we have seen from Matthew 5, 6 & 7! We are not listing who we think will enter the Kingdom of Heaven, but only who God says will enter

The Person Who Will Enter the Kingdom of Heaven

The person who is poor in spirit, those who are persecuted for the sake of Christ, those who practice the laws and commandments of God and those who do the will of the Father.

The first characteristic we find about those who will enter the Kingdom of Heaven is that they are: *"Poor in Spirit"*.

What does Matthew 5:3 say about the person who is poor in spirit? What word does He use to describe this person?

Blessed

If your answer was: *"they are blessed,"* then you answered correctly! God tells us that the person who is *"poor in spirit"* is the person who will enter His Kingdom and that they will be the person who is blessed. These two words: *"poor"* and *"blessed"* don't seem to go together, do they? Let's turn to our Word Window Section and look up the definition for *"blessed."* Once you've located the word definition for *"blessed,"* write down its meaning in the space provided. *Happy, supremely blessed, well off*

Blessed

_____

_____

_____

Based on the word meaning for *"blessed,"* how would you describe a person who is poor in spirit?

We see, just by looking at the word *"blessed,"* that Jesus begins His teaching session by describing to His audience what a happy person is like. This is the first of eight that Jesus will give to His listeners. Knowing what *"blessed"* means, we could read Matthew 5:3 this way: *"happy is the person who is poor in spirit."* I love the Amplified Bible translation for Matthew 5:3 that I've listed for you to read. Take a minute and ponder this translation.

Matthew 5:3 (Amplified)

"Blessed (happy, to be envied, and spiritually prosperous with life-joy and satisfaction in God's favor and salvation, regardless of their outward conditions) are the poor in spirit (the humble, who rate themselves insignificant), for theirs is the Kingdom of Heaven."

You can ask anyone today what makes them happy and you would find that there would be many different answers; many varying opinions. Why is this? It's because happiness means different things to different people. To some it's having the perfect job, a different husband or wife, the perfect body or the flawless face. It's having a certain amount of money, that expensive car or that 'must have' larger home. To some it's being physically or mentally well again. To some it's being loved by someone else. Generally speaking, in its basic form happiness is, a feeling of satisfaction or pleasure. It means having no sorrow or having the things you want. There are many who are in pursuit of happiness today, but there are few who find it.

You can turn on the TV today to any Christian network and it won't be long before you will find a message being delivered on, "happiness" or "blessings." A popular teaching today in Christendom is that God wants us to be happy and that He wants to bless us. The problem with this teaching is that often the happiness and the blessings from God are linked to prosperity or healing from sickness or disease. In other words our happiness, or the blessed life, is connected to our outward circumstances! According to Jesus' teaching in Matthew 5, 6 & 7, this view is not biblical. Another popular teaching is that happiness is a choice and it is found within each of us. We should put a smile on our face and go about our day! Well, this is great if we can go out and purchase a one-way ticket on the boat to happy land! Unfortunately this teaching is not biblical either, not according to Matthew 5, 6 & 7.

To help us fully appreciate this word, *"blessed,"* it will benefit us greatly to see how it is used throughout scripture. Look up the following verses that use this same word for *"blessed"* and write out what you learned from each. It's not so important that you note the details of the blessed life as much as it is that you see how this word is used. Keep in mind that the word *"blessed"* is God's word for true happiness.

- **I Timothy 1:11**

  conforms to the gospel glory of God

- **John 20:29**

  those who see Jesus & believes

- **Titus 2:13**

  Those who wait on Jesus

- **James 1:12**

  Those who persevere through hard times

- **Romans 4:7 & 8**

Just from the scriptures you looked at, how would you describe the person who is blessed or happy?

Would you say that the blessed life is based on outward circumstances? Explain your answer.

What did you learn about God in I Timothy 1:11?

We see in I Timothy 1:11, that God is a blessed God, a happy God! If God is blessed, or happy, wouldn't it make sense to say that happiness is found in being like God? In other words, happiness is found in having God-like qualities. You have just seen a most powerful truth, precious student. Happiness is not found without. It is never based on our surroundings, on our circumstances, or in others. This is totally opposite to what the world would say about finding

Happiness is found in having God like qualities.

happiness. Is it any wonder that when Jesus finished teaching, the people were amazed? Maybe you've been searching all your life for happiness and you've just not been able to find it. There are many women who suffer from depression and the number is rapidly climbing every year. It often leads to such despair in a woman's life that her relationships with others are destroyed, drug and alcohol addictions become a false source of happiness, and sometimes suicide seems the only way out. If you are one of these women or if you know someone who is, then grab hold of this truth, beloved student, and write it upon the tablet of your heart.

Principle
True happiness can only be found in a right relationship with God

This is a truth that secular counselors will not tell you, the world will not tell you and many popular teachings in Christendom will not tell you. It may sound harsh, but listen and take it to heart, beloved: **God is not interested in your happiness, He is interested in your holiness!** When you are holy, as He is holy, true happiness will flood into your life as you have never known. True happiness comes from character, God-like character, and nowhere else. You will never find it in self-worth, the approval of others, in position, relationships, materialism or money. The wellspring of happiness is found in His approval!

The life that is blessed is the life that is in a right relationship with God. Aren't you glad that true happiness is found only in a right relationship with God and that it is not found in our circumstances or in others? People will disappoint you and circumstances will rob you of your joy in a moment. Do you know what this truth means to you, precious student? Because true happiness is only found in a right relationship with God, then…

Benefit
Circumstances have no bearing on our happiness

Praise the Lord!! Aren't you glad, beloved student that happiness doesn't come from without? This is why you can see people who, though they are faced with tragic circumstances, can still have an inner joy that is unexplainable, even in the midst of great sorrow. You see, my dear companion, happiness was not meant to come and go, but to be a constant lifestyle of those who are in a right relationship with God. You may be asking what is that right relationship with God like, or what does it mean and how do I get it! These are all valid questions we will answer in the weeks to come, so hang in there with me and stay the course until you finish this study. This study will change your life if you will be a diligent student and apply its truths to your life. When God's word is applied to your life, your life cannot remain the way it was. But truth takes time, it is revealed a little here and a little there and truth will always build upon truth. So, be patient and you will reap the rewards of inductive Bible study in time.

You have just learned the first attribute of the blessed life. Take a minute and turn to the back of your study book and there you will find a chart entitled "The Blessed Life." Write down this first attribute on your chart. As we work through these chapters in Matthew, we will slowly fill in our chart until we have listed all eight. Your first one should read:

•*They are Poor in Spirit*

Every week we will have a memory verse that we will learn together. I have listed this week's verse below. Let's close out our time together today by reading over this verse three times, okay?

Isaiah 61:10

"I will rejoice greatly in the Lord,
My soul will exult in my God;
For He has clothed me with a robe of righteousness,
As a bridegroom decks himself with a garland,
And as a bride adorns herself with her jewels."

Day Two

Welcome back, beloved student, to another day of sitting at the feet of Jesus on a hill-side long ago, listening to His words written down for you and I to read in Matthew 5, 6 & 7. Before we get started, I want to ask you to take a minute and get on your knees before the Lord and ask Him to speak to you through His Word. Commit your time to Him that He may bless it. I will meet you back right here when you are finished talking with Him.

On Day One we began to see what those will be like who will enter the Kingdom of Heaven. We saw four characteristics about those who will enter God's Kingdom. For the sake of review, let's write out those four things once more so we will have a fresh start to today's study time. Look back to Day One if you need to.

Those Who Will Enter the Kingdom of Heaven

- *The poor in spirit*
- *Those who are persecuted for righteousness sake*
- *Those who practice and teach the commandments*
- *The one who does the will of the Father*

The first thing that we saw from this list was that those who are poor in spirit will enter the Kingdom of Heaven and that the poor in spirit are **"blessed" or "happy."** Yesterday we saw that true happiness comes from being in a right relationship with God. "Blessed are the poor in spirit," is the first of eight beatitudes that Jesus gives on this hillside to his listeners. This first one is the foundation stone upon which all the others are built. It's vital that we understand fully what Jesus meant when He said that those who are poor in spirit are blessed or they are happy. Before we can begin to fully understand true happiness, we must understand what it means to be *"poor in spirit."* This will be our focus of study today as we look at what it means to be poor in spirit.

To help refresh your memory, I want you to turn to our text of study, Matthew 5, 6 & 7 and read through these three chapters. Repetitive reading is more valuable than you can know when gleaning truths from God's Word. The more you read it the more it becomes united with your heart; the more you become one with the Word. Once you've finished reading the text I want to give you a challenge, so meet me back here in just a few minutes.

Challenge: You listed the four characteristics of those who will enter the Kingdom of Heaven. If I were to ask you to list the opposite characteristic of each of those, what would you write? For example if one characteristic was: "they would have love," then the opposite characteristic would be, "they have hate." Does this make sense? I have listed the four characteristics out for you; beside each one write the opposite of it. Don't rush this and make sure you take time to meditate on these as you list them.

Will Enter	**< Opposite >**	**Will Not Enter**
• Poor in spirit		• _____
• Persecuted for Righteousness		• _____
• Righteousness above Scribes & Pharisees		• _____
• Does the will of God		• _____

Based on the list you made, how would you describe the person who will not enter the Kingdom of God?

_____

_____

What did you write down for the opposite of *"poor in spirit?"*

_____

If I were to ask you what you think it means to be "poor in spirit," what would you write? You may be saying, "Pam, I have no idea!" I understand, it's okay not to know, but if you were to just think of the word "poor" and what it means, what do you think *"poor in spirit"* would mean? I really believe if you give it some thought, you can make an educated guess!

without a spirit, void of spirit

_____

THE BLESSED WOMAN

Let's look at what the word *"poor"* means. Turn to your Word Windows Section located in the back of your book and find the word *"poor"* and read its meaning. Once you've done that, come back and write down its definition in the space provided for you:

Poor

Pauper, destitute, beggar, poverty stricken.

It doesn't take long to see, as we read through these beatitudes that Jesus gives, that these are not natural qualities. They are not the norm. To be poor in spirit, we see, means to have a poverty of spirit, or to be one who cowers low because they are utterly destitute; they are powerless. For poverty to be present there must be the absence of wealth. For someone to have poverty of spirit means that they are without spirit; they are destitute of spirit. Read I Thessalonians 5:23 typed out below.

> *"Now may the God of peace Himself sanctify you entirely; and may your spirit and soul and body be preserved complete, without blame at the coming of our Lord Jesus Christ."*

According to this verse what are the three parts of man that Paul speaks of?

The _spirit_   *trichotomous (three part)*

The _soul_

The _body_

I believe, based on God's Word, that when God created man and woman, He created them body, soul and spirit. This is what is known as a trichotomous (three-part) being. Read Genesis 2:16-17 typed out for you.

Genesis 2:16-17

"¹⁶The Lord God commanded the man, saying, 'From any tree of the garden you may eat freely; ¹⁷But from the tree of the knowledge of good and evil you shall not eat, for in the day that you eat from it you will surely die.'"

According to verse 17 in this passage, what would happen to man or woman if they ate of the tree of knowledge of good and evil?

They would die

When Adam and Eve sinned (ate of the forbidden tree), they did not die physically, did they? They did not die physically nor did their souls die when they ate of the tree of the knowledge of good and evil. How then did they die? They must have died another way, for God said that they would die and God is not a liar. When Adam and Eve sinned, they hid themselves from God because they were suddenly aware of their condition; they were without clothing. Because man had sinned, God banished man from the garden and he was no longer able to have communion with God. It was at this point that man became destitute of spirit, or poor of spirit. When man sinned, he lost God's spirit. When man returns to God through Jesus Christ, he receives God's spirit, the Holy Spirit Who comes to reside in the heart of man.

To help you understand this truth, look up James 2:26 and write out what it says about the man without the spirit.

The body without a spirit is dead.

Do you see, precious student, that man apart from God is poor in spirit; he is absolutely destitute because he is without the living God. To help us better understand this truth, look up the following verses and write what you learned about being poor in spirit from each:

- **II Corinthians 6:10**

- **II Corinthians 8:9**

- **James 2:3-5**

- **Revelation 3:14-22**

There is a parable told by Jesus in Luke 18:9-14 that beautifully illustrates what it means to be poor in spirit. Take a minute and read through noting the reason why Jesus was giving this parable. Once you've finished reading write down in the space provided what you learned:

_____

_____

Why was Jesus giving this parable? What reason is given to us in verse 9?

_____

_____

Which person in this parable would you say is "poor in spirit"? Explain your answer.

_____

_____

Look up Romans 7:18 and write it out in the space provided.

Romans 7:18

_____

_____

_____

The apostle Paul was speaking in this passage. Would you say that Paul was "poor in spirit"? Explain your answer.

_____

_____

According to Matthew 9:10-13, what kind of people did Jesus come to call?

_____

_____

In Luke 4:18 Jesus is reading from Isaiah. According to what He read, who was the Gospel to be preached to?

_____

_____

Do you think that Jesus came to preach the Gospel to those who had no money, or could He have meant something else?

_____

_____

Jesus came to call those who needed Him. He came to proclaim the Gospel to all those who were *"poor in spirit;"* those who were without hope. Those who along with the tax collector, beat their chests and said, "God, be merciful to me the sinner." This is the heart of those who are *"poor in spirit."* Those who recognize that, without God, they are without hope, without spirit. This is why the first beatitude is the foundational stone upon which all the others are built. Man's first and foremost responsibility is this truth:

Principle
Man must recognize his spiritual poverty apart from God

This is the beginning point for all of mankind, beloved. It is here at this place that man recognizes that he needs God; that he will not make it without Him. And it's there in that moment of bowed knee to recognition of his sinfulness, that poverty of spirit is honored. It's not a recognition that you need God for something or even for someone, but it's recognizing that you need God

Himself. It is the cry of the humble that God's ears are attentive to. He despises the prideful heart. There is a difference in needing God for something and just needing God. Poverty of spirit is the absence of self-reliance, the absence of all pride. It is the deepest place of repentance. It is complete and utter brokenness. What do you think keeps us from recognizing, from seeing, our poverty of spirit? Look up the following verses and write out what you find that might keep us from recognizing our need for God in the space provided:

- **I Corinthians 1:18-22**

  _____

  _____

- **Romans 10: 1-3**

  _____

  _____

- **Matthew 19:16-24**

  _____

  _____

Things that blind us to seeing our "poverty of spirit":

_____

_____

_____

I believe that there are three basic things that keep us from seeing our "poverty of spirit:" **earthly wisdom, self-righteousness, and wealth or**

material things. These are all things that can blind us. These are the things that keep us from seeing our total depravity apart from God; but when man turns from these things and recognizes his total "poverty of spirit," a wonderful thing happens...

Benefit
He becomes rich

The pauper once in ragged garments is now clothed in garments of splendor and majesty. He who once lived on the filthy streets now walks down streets of purest gold. The beggar now sits at the King's table. The one who was in desperate need, now wants for nothing. He who had no future is now an heir to the throne of Heaven and he who had no home now resides in the palace of the majestic one. This is why Jesus said, *"Blessed is he who is poor in spirit, for his is the Kingdom of Heaven."* Poverty is a beautiful thing, isn't it, beloved?

It is here that we will finish our lesson for today, beloved. Read over our memory verse for the week and I will see you tomorrow! Love to you.

Day Three

What a week we've had so far, blessed student! We have reached Day Three of this week's study and we want to continue looking at the four characteristics of those who will enter the Kingdom of Heaven. As will be our practice, let's pause and bow our knee to the King of Heaven and seek His blessings as we study His precious Word. Once you've finished, we'll begin our study.

To refresh our memories, let's turn and read once again Matthew 5, 6 & 7. These chapters will become as a familiar and trusted friend to you by the time we have finished this study. Your life will never be the same having stored these precious verses in your heart and mind. Once you've finished I want you to write down the four characteristics of those who will enter the Kingdom of Heaven. You can look back on Day One or Day Two if you need to, but I believe you could probably write them from memory by now!

The Four Characteristics of Those Who Will Enter the Kingdom of Heaven

- _____
- _____
- _____
- _____

As you recall, we have looked at the first one; *"poor in spirit."* Today we want to look at the third characteristic. Don't worry, we will come back to the second characteristic on Day Four! These both deal with righteousness and so they will be studied side by side today and on Day Four. Write out below what these two characteristics are so there is no confusion.

- _____
- _____

Jesus told His listeners that the people who will enter the Kingdom of Heaven are those who have a righteousness that surpasses that of the Pharisees and Scribes and those who have been persecuted for this righteousness. For us to fully understand what Jesus is saying, let's look up the Greek definition for the word ***"righteousness"*** in our Word Window Section in the back of our book. Once you've found it, write it out in the space provided for you.

Righteousness

_____

_____

THE BLESSED WOMAN

I want you take a purple colored pencil and draw a circle around every reference to righteousness in Matthew 5, 6 & 7. I will give you a hint, the word righteousness is referred to five times in these chapters. See if you can find all five. Once you've finished, write out beside each verse what you learned about righteousness. I have listed these verses for you.

- **Matthew 5:6**

- **Matthew 5:10**

- **Matthew 5:20**

- **Matthew 6:1**

- **Matthew 6:33**

I believe that the major theme of the Sermon on the Mount is the lifestyle of the righteous who will enter the Kingdom of Heaven. It's this lifestyle that Jesus wants His audience, His followers, to understand. You can say the word "righteous" and most people will run for dear life with hands thrown up in disgust. Most people run either because they know they can't be righteous or because they simply don't want to be righteous. When Jesus taught this to the people, He was speaking to what had to be a predominantly Jewish audience. They understood righteousness as being a high standard of that few, if any, could ever reach. In their eyes, if anyone could attain righteousness, it would be the religious leaders of their day: the Scribes and Pharisees. So when Jesus said to them, *"Unless your righteousness exceeds that of the Scribes and Pharisees,"* you can imagine why they were in utter shock! How in the world could they do that?

By Jesus' time, the Pharisees and the Scribes had supreme influence among the people. They were in authority, teaching the Law and their interpretation of the Law. The people were at a disadvantage because they did not have their own copy of the Law to read for themselves. Because of this, they were at the mercy of their spiritual leaders not only to read the law to them, but also to teach and interpret it as well. The Pharisees and Scribes added their own ideas and words to the Law, teaching it to the people as divine words given to them by God. As a result of their influences, sin and righteousness had become something that was only an external act rather than a matter of the heart. This is why we see through the Sermon on the Mount the words, *"You have heard"... but I say to you."* Jesus was correcting the only teaching that the people had ever known. Jesus' words were contrary to everything they had ever been taught.

Let me summarize for you what Jesus taught them about true righteousness from the verses you looked up previously.

The righteousness that is needed to enter the Kingdom of Heaven:

1. We are to hunger and thirst for it
2. We will be persecuted because of it
3. It has to be greater than the righteousness of the religious leaders
4. We are not to practice it in front of others to be noticed
5. We are to seek it first above everything else

This was a pretty tall order, wouldn't you say? But how were they to obtain such righteousness? If you were to teach this message today in the Church, what do you think the response would be? Would there be any who would embrace this teaching? Most would walk away in dismay and shock knowing that they could never attain such a standard. The average churchgoer doesn't even want to stay in church past 12:00 noon let alone be persecuted for their beliefs! We put pastors, Christian leaders and evangelists on such pedestals today that we would not dare believe that we have to attain a level of righteousness that is above theirs! Isn't there supposed to be a higher standard for pastors than the layperson? Not according to Jesus' words, there isn't.

Look up Romans 3:10 and write it out below:

_____

_____

_____

What does it say about the righteous?

_____

_____

Though it is hard to swallow bare truth sometimes, beloved, let me ask you a question.

Do you have a righteousness that exceeds your spiritual leaders?

_____

_____

According to Jesus, if you don't have a righteousness that exceeds theirs will you enter the Kingdom of Heaven?

___

___

Are there any, including all spiritual leaders, who are righteous, according to Romans 3:10?

___

This is our Life Changing Principle for today's lesson:

Principle
Man's Righteousness Can Never Meet God's Standard

Jesus made it clear that there is a righteousness that man must have in order to enter the Kingdom of Heaven. It's a righteousness that surpasses perfection from man's point of view; a righteousness that would rejoice in the face of persecution. A righteousness that is not hypocritical, but pure and sincere. A righteousness that is to be valued above every other thing, even more than life itself. How could mankind ever achieve such a standard of righteousness? Would God demand of us a righteousness that we could never attain? This may sound harsh, but the answer is yes! He has every right to, beloved. God's righteousness is pure and holy and the standard of it cannot be lowered even for man. What God did do was something so amazing that the world would never be able to understand it. He became righteousness for us! The question becomes: Would God demand of us a righteousness that He would not provide for? The answer, beloved, is NO! To God be the glory.

Look up the following verses and write down what you learn about righteousness noting where true righteousness comes from. What a blessing these verses have been to me and I believe they will bless you as well, beloved daughter.

- Hosea 2:19-23

- Romans 10:9-10

- Matthew 9:13

- Galatians 3:6-11

According to the next few verses, where does our righteousness come from? From whom does it come? Write out your answer beside each.

- **I Corinthians 1:30**

_____

_____

- **Romans 8:10**

_____

_____

- **Titus 3:4-7**

_____

_____

Man can never attain the standard of righteousness that God required, but God did provide a place for man to find it. There is one place and one place only that righteousness can be found. We've seen in our principle that, "Man's Righteousness Can Never Meet God's Standard, but the good news for us, beloved daughter, is...

Benefit
Jesus' Righteousness Satisfied God's Demand

Oh, what a Savior! Oh, what a God! God would not demand a righteousness that He Himself would not meet! God cannot lower His standard, but He can raise you up to meet it! This is grace, beloved. This is grace in its purest form.

II Corinthians 5:21, beloved, should be your heart's praise song to Jesus. Read it and write out in the space provided what this verse means to you.

II Corinthians 5:21

"He made Him who knew no sin to be sin on our behalf, so that we might become the righteousness of God in Him."

_____

_____

_____

Aren't you glad that God didn't leave us helpless? God provided a way for man to come back to Him without lowering His standard! You see, daughter, God cannot remove His standard of holiness because He Himself is Holy and Holiness cannot act contrary to the Holy Word of God. Holiness cannot deny itself! Jesus became poor in spirit that you might become rich in spirit. Jesus put on sinful flesh that He might clothe you in garments of righteousness. What a marvelous Savior we have. Why don't you spend some time right now bowing your knee in total poverty before Him and worship Him. Thank Him and love Him for who He is and for what He has done for you. When was the last time you told Him how much you needed Him? This is how we will close our time together today. I am bowing on my knee with you as I write these last words. Thank you for loving Jesus enough to take this study. May He reap the glory, for He alone is worthy.

I will see you on Day Four.

Day Four

Welcome back! Take a few moments and pray, asking God to open your eyes that you may behold wonderful things from His Word. Dedicate your study time to Him and ask Him to give you an open ear to receive His truth. James 1:5 says, *"If any of you lacks wisdom, let him ask of God, who gives to all generously and without reproach, and it will be given to him."* So ask God for wisdom and put your faith in Him, and in Him alone, to teach you His Word.

Now that you've prayed, let's get started today by reading through Matthew 5, 6 & 7.

So far this week we have seen the four characteristics of those who will enter the Kingdom of Heaven. We know from God's Word that those who will enter the Kingdom of Heaven will be: poor in spirit, have a righteousness that surpasses that of the Scribes and Pharisees, persecuted for righteousness, and they will do the will of the Father. Today we will look at these last two characteristics. We have already seen from our study time together on Day Three that true righteousness can only come through Jesus Christ. This righteousness that comes through Jesus will not only allow us to enter into the Kingdom of Heaven, but it will also bring persecution for us while we are here on this earth.

Look up the following verses and list what you learn about persecution beside each:

- **John 15:20**

_____

_____

- **II Corinthians 4:9**

_____

_____

- **II Timothy 3:10-12**

_____

_____

- **Galatians 6:12**

_____

_____

According to these verses, who will be persecuted?

_____

_____

Do you believe Christians are persecuted for their beliefs today? Why or why not?

_____

_____

We could ask just about any Christian today what their idea of persecution is and we would get a variety of answers. Some believe that persecution only involves physical sufferings such as beatings or imprisonments. Others may include verbal abuse as well as the physical sufferings. Still others may agree that persecution may include not only physical and verbal abuse, but emotional, which can come in a lot of different ways. It may mean that you don't get that job promotion, that you lose a friendship or maybe even lose a spouse. I do think we would all agree that persecution can come in different packages and from one degree to another. Some forms of persecution are more extreme than others often bringing death.

The question I have for you beloved is: do you think Christians are persecuted today? If so, list some ways that you think Christians are persecuted around the World today? Include your own country and the ways that persecution may be exhibited.

Forms of Persecution for the Christian Today

There are many dear believers around the world who are suffering for their faith. Let me share one of these stories with you. This is real and it has happened just recently during the writing of this study.

In a small Sudan village, there was a faithful group of believers; about five families in all. They would meet secretly in their homes, praising and worshiping God together every week. They decided to have a Bible study for the local children of village and asked them to come to a meeting one night. They knew that this might cost them their very lives, but they believed with all of their heart that God was leading them to do this. The local authorities found out about it and raided the homes of all these families, dragging the men out and beating them in the streets.

They hauled them off to prison where they kept them for many days, torturing them relentlessly and demanding that they deny Christ if they wanted to live. Every time they were asked to deny Jesus, the men asked, *"How can we deny our Lord and Savior? He died for us that we may live with Him."* After many weeks these men died from starvation and torture. Their wives were interviewed and asked what they would do now that their husbands were dead. Their reply, full of faith, was, *"We will continue on with the work of the Lord until He calls us home as well."* What a powerful testimony of a relentless heart, a steadfast faith. They were willing to pay any price so that Christ might live in them in all His glory.

You see, beloved, persecution is very real and it is a very active force against devout Christians today all around the world. There are those who are truly "striving for the faith of the Gospel;" men and women whom the world is not worthy of. Jesus wanted His followers to know that following Him,

THE BLESSED WOMAN

believing in Him, would have a price and for some it could even mean death. Jesus wants us to know the whole truth, not just the easy truth. It's easy to accept the teachings that God is love and God is a God who forgives; that He is a God who hears us when we call and will provide for our needs. Persecution is a far cry from, "give us this day our daily bread!" We don't want to hear the words: "We will be persecuted if we choose to live godly." Most Christians will quit serving God when their feelings are hurt or when they feel unappreciated. We will throw up our hands and say, "It's just not worth it," at the first sign of any trouble. Persecution, no, we don't want anything to do with persecution. If we can't take challenges within the Church, how will we ever withstand persecution from the world?

I believe the answer is found in the last characteristic of the one who will enter the Kingdom of Heaven. Will you find it and write it out below? Look back from our previous days if you need to.

The one who will enter the Kingdom of Heaven will be persecuted, but they will do the will of the Father. These two attributes go hand in hand. When you do the will of the Father you will be persecuted. But, the one who does the will of the Father will also be the person who is *"happy,"* or *"blessed."* This is a far cry from a lot of the preaching that is heard on television and on the radio! Happy is the person who does the will of the Father and the one who does the will of the Father will be persecuted! How can we be happy if we are being persecuted?

Turn to your Word Window Section and look up the word meaning for *"persecuted"* and write it out in the space provided.

Persecuted

What do you think it means to do the will of the Father?

_____

_____

Look up the following verses on the will of God and write out any insights that you glean beside each.

- **I Peter 4:19**

_____

_____

- **I John 2:17**

_____

_____

- **Ephesians 6: 5-6**

_____

_____

- **Ephesians 5:17**

_____

_____

- **Ephesians 1:11**

_____

_____

- **John 6:39-40**

_____

_____

- **Matthew 12:50**

_____

_____

We see from these verses that God's will is real and He is working to bring about all that His will desires upon this earth. Jesus did the will of God and all those who belong to God will also do the will of God. There is no mistaking this in scripture. Doing the will of God means living a Godly or a God-like life or a life of righteousness. Do you remember what II Timothy 3:10-12 said? Take a minute and write it out below. It bears repeating, beloved.

- **II Timothy 3:10-12**

_____

_____

_____

Doing the will of God, beloved, comes with a price, doesn't it? That is why a Godly life is a rare find in the world today. It is not popular to live Godly, to live righteously, nor is it comfortable.

Principle
The Life Lived for God Will Face Persecution

Persecution can be perilous at times and can be difficult to understand. We read stories of whole families, including women and children, who were tortured and killed in the vilest of ways all because they chose to live for Jesus. Our hearts are gripped and in our flesh we cry out, "why?" Why must innocent people be treated in such a way? Understanding persecution is impossible from a human perspective. This is because God never intended for us to understand it through eyes of flesh! Persecution is a tolerance by God that allows evil men to do evil against His children, but only for a season. It's in this season of tolerance that great glory is given to God. For it is only when the petal of rose is crushed that its sweet fragrance is released. When a seed dies and is planted in the ground, it multiplies! If left just a seed it will never bring forth fruit. This is the beauty of persecution, beloved. When we choose to do the will of God, for we can do nothing less as His children, persecution will come. But with the coming of persecution, we can know...

Benefit
The Life That is Lived for God is the Life That Wins

Why is this, beloved? It's because the life that lives for God is the life that can never be separated from Him. Nothing can separate you from Him! This is the life that will someday grace the victor's crown.! Persecution will come, but with it will come a day of God's reward and of God's judgment against all those who persecuted His beloved children. Write this second beatitude in The Blessed Life Chart.

We've seen so much just in our first week together! Let's review the Principles and Benefits we've learned this week.

Week in Review

Principle # 1: *True happiness can only be found in a right relationship with God*
Benefit: *Circumstances have no bearing on our happiness*

Principle # 2: *Man must recognize his spiritual poverty apart from God*
Benefit: *He becomes rich*

Principle #3: *Man's righteousness can never meet God's standard*
Benefit: *Jesus righteousness satisfied God's demand*

Principle #4: *The life that is lived for God will face persecution*
Benefit: *The life that is lived for God is the life that wins*

In closing, I want to ask you a few questions to help you search your heart regarding the truths we have learned this week. Take your time and answer them as honestly as you can. This is between you and your Heavenly Father.

Personal Evaluation

Do you have the four characteristics of those who will enter the Kingdom of God?

Are you poor in spirit? Do you recognize that you need God?

Is your lifestyle characterized by doing the will of God?

Is your righteousness genuine or do you do righteous acts just to be noticed by others?

Review your memory verse, beloved, and see if you can write it out without looking.

_____

_____

_____

Well, you have finished your first week of *"The Blessed Life."* I am so very proud of you. The truths that we have learned this week have not been easy ones and so I have prayed for you ahead of time that God will cause your heart to not only see truth, but to embrace truth. Truth is meaningless in your life if you do not embrace it, beloved. This is only the beginning of Jesus' powerful message that He shared that day on a hillside over two thousand years ago. Even I stand in awe of His powerful convicting words. They have and are continuing to change my life day by day. Stay the course, beloved student; stay on this mountain with me until we have heard every word that the Lord wanted His people to hear that day so very long ago.

I will see you in our lesson time together! Much love to you.

Pam

LESSON TWO
Blessed Are They Who Mourn

Day One

    How well I remember the day that I received Jesus Christ as my Lord and Savior. I had been attending a small church in our hometown and God had been convicting me of my sins for several weeks. I was only 17 years old at the time but my life was full of many regrets and deep sadness from the guilt of living a sinful life. Finally, on Mother's Day, 1981, I could bare it no more. I ran down the aisle and fell on my knees at the altar sobbing uncontrollably. I didn't care what others were thinking; I only wanted to get to God. There in that little church, down on my knees before God, I grieved over my sins. Tears of great sorrow fell upon the steps that morning but they also fell at the feet of a merciful and loving Father. It was as if someone had died in my heart for I was grieved over the sins I had committed and I was even more grieved that I had hurt the heart of God. It was truly a time of mourning for I saw myself as God saw me. Mourning is not a subject most of us want to become familiar with, yet it is a certainty of life for most.

    Have you ever mourned beloved, truly mourned over something or someone? Maybe you've seen someone who has truly mourned over a great loss or situation. Would you describe someone who is mourning by using the word *"blessed"* or *"happy?"* Happy would be the last word we would use to describe someone who was mourning, but yet Jesus used this word to describe the mourner. What could He possibly have meant when He looked out into the crowd that day and said: "Happy is the person who mourns." How can a person who mourns be happy? Out of all the *"blessed,"* this one is probably the most difficult to understand. How can a person be considered a blessed person if they are mourning? This is not the attitude of the world today, is it? It's certainly not a predominant truth that is taught in our Churches today and it's definitely not embraced by most professing Christians. In fact, the opposite teaching that "God wants to bless you," occurs in many places today. If this is true, then based on Matthew 5:5 we could say, "God wants us to mourn." Jesus clearly taught that the one who mourns is the one who is blessed. Blessing and mourning go hand in hand according to Jesus. Many people will say they want to be blessed, but not many would say they want to mourn! *"Blessed are they who mourn"* is Jesus' second beatitude and the one that we will study this week, precious student. Remember to pray before you begin.

Take a few minutes and read through our main text of study (Matthew 5, 6 & 7) and then I will meet you back right here.

Now that you've finished reading our passage of study, I want you to write out this second beatitude in the space provided for you. I have started it for you.

"Blessed are those who _____

_____

Turn to your Word Window Section and look up the definition for "**mourn**" as used here in Matthew 5:5. Once you've found it write out its definition in the space provided.

Mourn

_____

_____

_____

Based on the definition of this word, write a description of the person who mourns in your own words.

The Person Who Mourns

So far we've seen that the word mourn that it means a mourning that is deep. It is not just sadness but it is a deep grief of heart, one that is all encompassing, meaning it affects every part of the person's life. This word means to mourn for, or to lament, as a way of life. Look up the following verses that use this same word for mourn as found in **Matthew 5:5** and write down what you learned about mourning from each.

- **Matthew 9:14-15**

- **Luke 6:25**

- **James 4:8-9**

Look up the following verses on mourning that are found in the Old Testament and record what you learn.

- **Job 5:11**

- **Isaiah 61:2**

- **Jeremiah 4:27-28**

From the verses we've read so far, we begin to see that there are many reasons why people mourn and there are degrees of mourning. Have you ever wondered who the first person was that mourned, beloved? Where did mourning begin? Let me take you to the first passage in scripture where we see that a heart was grieved or that a heart mourned. Note who it was and what they were mourning over.

- **Genesis 6:1-6**

_____

_____

_____

Did you see it, beloved? Mourning was birthed in the heart of God before it was ever birthed in the heart of man. God's heart was the first to ever mourn. What did God's heart mourn over?

_____

_____

To know that God's heart was the first heart that grieved and it was grieved because of the sins of man should cause us to grieve. Has your life ever grieved the heart of God, daughter? Has God ever mourned over you? I want us to look at Isaiah 53:1-6 together. These verses refer to Jesus Christ and they are typed out for you. Take a moment and read through them prayerfully. Once you've done that, I want you to go back through this passage once more. Only this time, draw a circle around every reference to grief or sorrow.

Isaiah 53:1-6

¹Who has believed our message? And to whom has the arm of the LORD been revealed?
²For He grew up before Him like a tender sheep, and like a root out

of parched ground; He has no stately form or majesty that we should look upon Him, nor appearance that we should be attracted to Him.

³He was despised and forsaken of men, A man of sorrows and acquainted with grief; and like one from whom hide their face He was despised, and we did not esteem Him.

⁴Surely our griefs He Himself bore, and our sorrows He carried; yet we ourselves esteemed Him stricken, smitten of God, and afflicted.

⁵But He was pierced through for our transgressions, He was crushed for our iniquities; the chastening for our well-being fell upon Him, and by His scourging we are healed.

⁶All of us like sheep have gone astray, each of us have turned to his own way; but the LORD has caused the iniquity of us all to fall on Him.

From your markings, write out a description of the life of Jesus.

Jesus

Grief was a way of life for Jesus and He was "blessed" because He mourned. He mourned because His Heavenly Father mourned. Jesus was one with His Father and His heart was an absolute replication of the heart of God for He was God. When we think of God we think of strength and power beyond anything we could ever imagine. God created the heavens and the earth. He drew the boundaries for the great waters and they cannot cross them unless He allows them too. He holds every star in its place and they cannot fall unless He Himself releases them from His mighty hands. He commands the sun to rise and set and there is nothing beyond His control or out of His grip. Knowing how powerful and mighty God is, how can it be that He would ever grieve over man, who is made of flesh and blood? Yet, He does. Strength and power are no stranger to grief. As mighty as God is, His heart is not exempt from grief because He has a heart of flesh like you and me, yet holy and pure. His heart beats just as yours and mine does, it experiences sadness, pain, anger and joy, yet He is God. What an unexplainable God we have precious daughter. To understand what it means to mourn, you must understand where it originated. This brings us to a powerful, heart moving principle…

Principle
Mourning finds its birthplace in the heart of God

How marvelous and unfathomable our God is. Aren't you glad that God understands what it means to grieve, to be sorrowful, to mourn? How can we ever relate to a God that cannot relate to us? Turn to Hebrews 4:15 and write out what you learn about Jesus, our High Priest. Jesus and God are one, so what is true of one is true of the other.

- **Hebrews 4:15**

_____

_____

_____

We not only have a God who can empathize with us but we also have a Savior who can as well. Heaven understands mourning because the heart of God rules over the Heavens and He is a God who understands you and I better than we understand ourselves. God the Father and God the Son have revealed to us the depth of grief and pain. Because this is true, beloved, we can now know what it means to mourn, to grieve. If God Himself mourned—If Jesus, His only begotten Son mourned— then shouldn't we mourn also? Because mourning was birthed in the heart of God, oh daughter, the following is true…

Benefit
A pattern for mourning is given

Because God mourned, beloved, we are also to mourn for we are to be like Him in all things. If God is not exempt from grieving then neither are we. Because He mourned so are we to mourn. God set the standard for us to follow. Look up the following scripture and write it out in the space provided. Although it may not, at first glance, seem to fall into line with mourning, you will come to see how beneficial this verse is with the truths we will learn this week. It is our memory verse for this week. Read it aloud several times so that you may begin to memorize the verse in the storehouse of your heart.

MEMORY VERSE
Ecclesiastes 3:14

_____

_____

_____

_____

Well, you've worked so very hard precious, I am so proud of you! Let's close our time together today by writing out what you learned about God today.

What I learned about God...

_____

_____

_____

_____

I will see you on Day Two!

Day Two

What a day we had yesterday, precious student. I have prayed for you that today would be even more spiritually beneficial as we journey a little deeper into the life of one who mourns. We learned yesterday that the act of mourning originated in the heart of God. I remember the first day God revealed this to me. I was so shocked to learn that God was the first one who ever had His heart broken. How could I have not known this truth all the years I had been saved? What a deep work and teaching that God has begun in me and still continues to do through this truth. To teach on mourning in the Church today is almost unheard of because it doesn't appeal to our flesh.

We know that we are to mourn, but what are we to mourn over? This will be our topic of study today. Take time to pray and I will meet you when you are finished.

Can you imagine what the people could have been thinking that day as Jesus sat on the hillside and said these words to them: *"Blessed are those who mourn, for they shall be comforted."* Surely these words sounded strange and untrue to the listeners as they tried to understand within themselves how they could mourn and yet be blessed at the same time. Would you consider someone who was in mourning to be a blessed person? Most of us would probably have to answer, "no" to that question. But you see, precious student, what I believe Jesus was saying that day long ago was that the blessing is not found in the mourning, but in the comfort that comes from God in the midst of the mourning. I'll never forget the day that God spoke to my heart during a time of great darkness in my life; a time of great suffering as I questioned why and this is what he spoke to my heart: *"How can I be your song in the night if I never allow the night to come?"*

Beloved, we are to mourn and in that mourning we can know the comfort of our Heavenly Father in a way that we could not have any other way. It's during these times of mourning that we become intimate with God, intimate with our sweet Savior. But what are we to mourn over? Does God expect us to go around in perpetual mourning and weeping? What kind of mourning was Jesus referring to? This is the question that we want to begin looking at in our study time together and for the remainder of this week's study.

I believe that we, as Christians, are to mourn over three things. We will look at one today and the other two on the remaining two days we have together. Find in your Bible Luke 7 and read verses 37-50. Write down in the space provided for you the reason we see mourning taking place.

- **Luke 7: 37-50**

_____

_____

Let's read through this passage once more, but this time take a colored pencil of your choice and draw a circle around every reference to the woman. Be sure and circle all the pronouns for her as well. Once you are finished, go back and review every place you marked a reference to the woman. With these in mind, answer the following questions.

Why was this woman weeping?

_____

_____

How would you describe this woman from what we see in this passage?

_____

_____

What was her attitude toward sin?

_____

What was her attitude toward the Lord?

_____

THE BLESSED WOMAN

Would you say that this woman had a heart that truly grieved over her sin?

Every time I read this account I am filled with empathy for this woman, for I can understand the love she had for the Lord. Like this woman, I, too, was so sinful the day that I came and fell at His feet wanting only to be forgiven, wanting only to find peace for my sin sick soul. This woman wept over her sin because she saw her sin through the eyes of God. Over two thousand years have passed since this woman wept at the feet of Jesus yet her tears are remembered as if they were yesterday. Forgiveness is made fresh through her life for us who understand what it means to have been forgiven. This woman sought peace that day but instead she was given the Prince of Peace. This kind of mourning moves the heart of the Lord. May the cry of our heart beloved be: *"Oh God, break my heart with the things that break Your heart."*

I want us to take the remainder of our day together studying Psalm 38. I believe it is one of the most powerful passages on the effects of sin in the Word of God. It is typed out for you below. Take time to read through this passage slowly so that you take it all in. There are many truths found in these precious verses for they open up to us the heart of one who is truly grievous over their sin.

Psalm 38:1-18

[1] Oh Lord, rebuke me not in Your wrath, and chasten me not in Your burning anger.

[2] For Your arrows have sunk deep into me.

[3] There is no soundness in my flesh because of Your indignation; There is no health in my bones because of my sin.

[4] For my iniquities are gone over my head; as a heavy burden they weigh too much for me.

[5] My wounds grow foul and fester because of my folly

[6] I am bent over and greatly bowed down; I go mourning all day long.

[7] For my loins are filled with burning, and there is no soundness in my flesh.

[8] I am benumbed and badly crushed; I groan because of the agitation of my heart.

⁹Lord, all my desire is before You, and my sighing is not hidden from You.

¹⁰My heart throbs, my strength fails me; and the light of my eyes, even that has gone from me.

¹¹My loved ones and my friends stand aloof from my plague; and my kinsmen stand afar off.

¹²Those who seek my life lay snares for me; and those who seek to injure me have threatened destruction, and they devise treachery all day long.

¹³But I, like a deaf man, do not hear; and I am like a mute man who does not open his mouth.

¹⁴Yes, I am like a man who does not hear, and in whose mouth are no arguments.

¹⁵For I hope in You, oh Lord; You will answer, oh Lord my God.

¹⁶For I said, "May they not rejoice over me, Who, when my foot slips, would magnify themselves against me."

¹⁷For I am ready to fall, and my sorrow is continually before me.

¹⁸For I confess my iniquity; I am full of anxiety because of my sin.

Now that you've read through this passage once, read through it again, but this time mark every reference to the writer by drawing a box around them in the color of your choice. Choose a nice bold color so it will easily stand out for you. Once you've finished, make a list of the things you learned about the writer in the space provided. This is done very easily by going back to each place you drew a box and see what is said about the writer.

About the Writer

From the list you made, how would you describe this person?

_____

_____

_____

What was the problem this person was having? What was the cause of his condition?

_____

_____

What was his heart's attitude toward his sin?

_____

_____

How did sin affect this man's life? Remember to go back to your markings and note what you find there about the effects of sin.

_____

_____

_____

_____

You see, beloved, sin is costly to anyone who allows it to come into their lives either by their own doing or at the influence and hands of others. Sin affects every aspect of our lives. This brings us to a powerful principle, beloved…

Principle
Sin mars life

Did you see the depths of the effects of sin in this person's life that we read about in Psalm 38? It affected their heart, their health, and relationships with their friends and families; it affected their emotional state and even changed their countenance. It made them anxious and their heart was in constant turmoil. When we recognize the effects of sin in our lives and how our sin grieves the heart of God, I believe we begin to understand why we should grieve over our personal sins.

Go back to Psalm 38 and find Verse 10. Write it out below in the space provided.

_____

_____

What had gone from his eyes?

_____

From this verse we see that life is changed or marred because of sin. We also see that even the light in the eyes had gone out. Now, in the light of this truth, turn to our main passage of study and read Matthew 5:14-16.

According to these verses, when the light is seen by others, what will it do?

_____

_____

Turn to your Word Windows Section and find the definition for **"Light"** as used here in Matthew 5:14 & 16 and write its meaning out below in the space provided.

Light

_____

_____

You see, beloved, light was meant to be manifested. We are to let our light shine in such a way that God is glorified because the light will always glorify the Father. Darkness comes with the sin, preventing the light from being seen. If the light cannot be seen, then the Father cannot be glorified. This is why we are to mourn over our sins: because God is not glorified.

Sin mars a life from the form that God intended it to be. Because Sin mars life, then the following is true…

Benefit
God's glory is hidden

Everything has its wages, precious student, and although God's glory being hidden is not in any way a benefit to us as believers, it most certainly is a benefit to Satan. Satan's desire is to hide God from the world and when we allow sin in our lives he gets his heart's desire. Because sin mars life, precious student, then that which God intended to be seen is hidden. God created us in His very image that His glory may be shown throughout all of creation. You are the only part of creation that God imprinted Himself with. You are to be the very imprint of God to the world. Very convicting, isn't it? I understand. We, as God's children, have a tremendous responsibility of how we are to live our lives. Sin is not to be present and if it is, we are to deal with it immediately because it keeps the glory of God from being seen. Sin veils the glory of God when it is present in our lives.

Last but not least, let's review our memory verse together. Oh, the priceless benefits of scripture memorization. Once the word is tucked away in your heart it is there forever! Your heart becomes the very storehouse of the Word of God. Let's take a moment and write out our memory verse for this week in the space below. This will help you memorize your verse.

MEMORY VERSE
Ecclesiastes 3:14

_____

_____

_____

_____

Just to sum up our truths for the day, beloved. I leave you with this question...

If sin is present in our lives, how will the world ever see the glory of the Father?

_____

_____

This, beloved, is why we should mourn.

You've worked hard today in our study time together and I am so proud of you. I know these lessons are difficult to bear and I want you to know that I have prayed for you before this study ever came to be in your hands. How I have asked the Lord to transform your life so that your light will so shine before men that they may glorify the Father who is in Heaven. You were created to shine, formed by the hands of God to radiate His image so that the world may know Him. Why don't you take some time to go to God in prayer asking Him to search your heart and reveal any sin that might be present. I John 1:9 tells us that when we confess our sins, He is just and faithful to forgive us of those sins.

I will see you on Day Three.

Day Three

Welcome back to another day of being in God's Word together. Yesterday we studied one of the three things we are to mourn over as God's children. Do you remember what it was? Today, we are going to open up God's Word and learn about the second one. Take time to pray before you begin if you haven't done so already. Remember, truth is not obtained, it must be revealed, so ask the Holy Spirit to reveal truth to your heart and mind as you study God's Word. I will meet you back here.

Let's begin by reading through our main passage of study found in Matthew Chapters 5-7. I know these chapters are long, but there is nothing more beneficial than repetitive reading of God's Word. It will soak in a little deeper each time you read through it.

Write out below the beatitude we have been studying this week.

"*Blessed are those who*_____

_____"

I want us to look at Revelation 2:18-29 today. It is typed out for you. Take time to read through it once and then we will mark some key words together.

Revelation 2:18-29

[18] "And to the angel of the church of Thyatira write: The Son of God, who has eyes like a flame of fire, and His feet are like burnished bronze, says this:
[19] I know your deeds, and your love and faith and service and perseverance, and that your deeds of late are greater than at first.
[20] 'But I have this against you, that you tolerate the woman Jezebel, who calls herself a prophetess, and she teaches and leads My bond-servants astray so that they commit acts of immorality and eat things sacrificed to idols.
[21] 'I gave her time to repent, and she does not want to repent of her immorality.
[22] 'Behold, I will throw her on a bed of sickness, and those who commit adultery with her into great tribulation, unless they repent of her deeds.
[23] 'And I will kill her children with pestilence, and all the churches will know that I am He who searches the minds and hearts' and I will give to each one of you according to your deeds.
[24] 'But I say to you, the rest who are in Thyatira, who do not hold this teaching, who have not known the deep things of Satan, as they call them— I place no other burden on you.

²⁵'Nevertheless what you have, hold fast until I come.

²⁶'He who overcomes, and he who keeps My deeds until the end, TO HIM I WILL GIVE AUTHORITY OVER THE NATIONS;

²⁷AND HE SHALL RULE THEM WITH A ROD OF IRON, AS THE VESSELS OF THE POTTER ARE BROKEN TO PIECES, as I also have received authority from my Father;

²⁸And I will give him the morning star.

²⁹'He who has an ear, let him hear what the Spirit says to the Churches."

According to Verse 29, to whom is the Spirit speaking?

Who is to listen to what the Spirit is saying to the churches? What kind of person?

I know this seems like a silly answer, but if your answer was anyone who has an ear then you were correct. In fact, the scripture doesn't even say we have to have two ears, just AN ear! Interesting, isn't it? Let me ask you something, beloved: Do you have an ear? If so, then we are to listen to what the Spirit is saying to the Churches. Let's do some markings of key words in this passage and find out what the Spirit is saying to the Churches, okay?

Take a colored pencil of your choice and mark every reference to the Church of Thyatira by drawing a blue box around each. Remember to include any pronouns as well. Once you've finished, make a list of everything you learned about this Church in the space provided.

Church of Thyatira

Were there any good things that this Church was doing? If so, what were they?

_____

_____

_____

What did the Lord have against this Church?

_____

_____

Take a colored pencil of your choice and underline every reference to Jezebel.

Make a list of everything you learned about this woman from marking the text.

Jezebel

_____

_____

_____

Based on what we've seen so far, could we safely say that this Church was in sin?

_____

If you answered yes, then you are absolutely right, beloved. This Church was a Church that was tolerating sin. What was God calling for this Church to do because of this sin?

_____

Turn to your Word Windows Section and look up the definition for **"tolerate"** as found in verse 20 and record it below. The word for **"tolerate"** in the King James Version is "sufferest" and it is the only place in the Word of God that this particular word is used.

Tolerate

_____

_____

What were the people tolerating in their church?

_____

_____

What was this woman doing that was wrong?

_____

_____

By allowing this woman to do the things she was doing in the Church they were tolerating sin in their midst. Beloved, the Church is never to tolerate sin.

Based on the meaning of the word "tolerate" (sufferest), what do you think it means to tolerate sin?

___

___

Every time sin is tolerated we become a little more desensitized to it until, in time, there no longer remains a conscience of sin. What was going to happen to this Church as a result of tolerating sin? Read the passage carefully and see if you can glean any insights to the impending consequences of their tolerance of sin. Record your answer in the space provided.

___

___

Do you see, beloved student, why the Church cannot tolerate sin? There are grave consequences for any group of people who tolerate sin.

Look up Proverbs 14:34 and write what you learn about sin.

___

Turn to your Word Windows Section and look up the meaning of **"reproach"** and record it in the space provided.

Reproach

_____

_____

In the light of this meaning, let me ask you a very pointed question. Can the Church tolerate sin and glorify God at the same time?

_____

Though this may sound harsh, beloved, any Church that tolerates sin dishonors God. This is the message that I believe God is giving to the Church in our generation. The Church is being beckoned by God to repent and return to Him with a heart of humility and sincerity. The Church cannot show the glory of God to a lost and dying world when God's glory doesn't exist within it. Knowing this, beloved, we see our principle for today...

Principle
God is dishonored when sin is present

A holy God cannot be present where there is sin and He can never be glorified. We have seen this very clearly from the Church at Thyatira, but remember, this message was for the Churches! This message was not just for this one Church, but also rather for all the Churches of God. What a vital message for us today. This should break our hearts, beloved. Sin present in the Church should bring about mourning in the hearts of God's people. The heart's desire of the Church should be to glorify God in all that it says and in all that it does. Most of all, sin in the Church breaks the very heart of God because God will have to deal with it, for He cannot deny Himself and He cannot tolerate sin in the Church.

Let's look at one more Church, beloved. It's found in I Corinthians 5:1-13. Take a moment and read through this chapter and answer the questions below.

THE BLESSED WOMAN

What was happening in this Church?

_____

_____

What was the Church's attitude toward sin?

_____

_____

Were they to tolerate the sin that was present?

_____

_____

Would there be consequences if they did not deal with the sin that was present within their Church? If so, what were they?

_____

_____

Are we to judge sin in the Church, according to these verses?

_____

_____

Didn't we see that there were consequences to their sin? When sin is present in the life of a Church, or a person, or group of persons, God must deal with it accordingly. God cannot, nor will he, dismiss our sin. The Lord is to be Lord over His Church because it bears His name. He will always call for repentance because He is over the Church. This brings us to the benefit of our principle today…

Benefit
God is not in His proper place

There is a price for any sin, a benefit that we reap as a result of it, though painful as it is. You may be saying right now, "Pam, the Church would never just choose to dishonor God and they certainly would never want God to be out of place." But you see, precious daughter, every time the Church tolerates sin and does not deal with it according to God's word, they are making a choice to dishonor God. It's the same way in our personal lives. We are not only to mourn over our personal sins, but we are to mourn over sin in the Church. Let me ask you a question:

When was the last time you wept over sin in the Church? Have you ever wept over sin in the Church?

_____

As a result of our study today, why do you think the Church needs to be diligent in guarding itself against Sin?

_____

_____

Do you believe that we should mourn over sin in the Church and if so, why do you think we should mourn over sin in the Church?

_____

_____

_____

As we close our time together, beloved, turn to your memory verse found in Ecclesiastes and review it so you will have it stored in your heart. You have worked so hard today and you we have learned some difficult things. The truths you are learning are not popular, but they are God's truth and they are God's heart for us and for the Church. Truth that is not embraced and lived out is truth that is rejected and thrown to the way side. My prayer is for the Church of God and for His people to rise up and repent of sin and seek the forgiveness of God that they may bring the honor that He so justly deserves.

I want to leave you with a challenge that I've given to you already in this week's study.

CHALLENGE

Will you begin to pray daily this prayer?

"God, break my heart with the things that break your heart."

See you on Day Four! Much love to you….

Day Four

Wow! We are already on our last day of Lesson Two! What a wonderful, diligent student you've been thus far. I'm so proud of you! Have I told you that lately? I really am so proud of you and oh, how God's heart is just rejoicing over you, daughter, for setting your heart to study His precious Word. Isn't a wonderful feeling to know that what you are doing is bringing pleasure to God? Are you ready? Let's get started, but before you do, take time to get on your knees and ask God to teach you truth through His Holy Spirit. God's desire is for us to know truth and He will not withhold it from His children who diligently seek after it.

Let's begin by reading once more through our text of study found in Matthew Chapters 5, 6, & 7. Remember, repetition is so important in studying God's Word. Once you're finished, I will meet you back here.

Now that you've read through the text, let's review what we've learned thus far. Write out below the beatitude that we have been studying this week.

"Blessed are _____ *"*

So far, we've learned that we are to mourn and we've learned two things that we are to mourn over. Can you list what they are below?

We are to mourn over _____

We are to mourn over _____

If you answered that we are to mourn over sin in our lives and sin in the Church, then you were right! Today, we want to see the third thing we are to mourn over according to God's Word. Remember, beloved, that mourning is to be a way of life. Our main text of study today is found in Ezekiel Chapter 9. The book of Ezekiel was written during the time when the Babylonians took Judah, the Southern Kingdom, captive. Judah had been taken captive because God was judging them according to their sins. They had forsaken God's commandments and God was calling them to repentance, but the people had not listened. There was still a remnant of people living in Jerusalem who had not been taken into captivity for God had not completely destroyed the city. But God was giving one final call to His people to repent and return to Him. Turn in your Bible and read through this passage and answer the following questions.

According to this passage, who was to draw near?

_____

_____

What were they to bring in their hands when they came?

_____

_____

What were the executioners to do? (hint: it's found in Verses 5 & 6)

_____

_____

According to Verses 3-4, what was the man in linen to do?

_____

_____

_____

Why do you think he was to do this; what purpose did this serve?

_____

_____

Describe the state of the people in this passage.

_____

_____

What would you say their attitude toward sin was?

_____

_____

Who would be exempt from the judgment God was sending through the executioners?

_____

_____

It was only the mourners who would be spared, beloved. Why? Because God said, *"Blessed are those who mourn, for they shall be comforted."* The blessing is not found in the mourning, but rather in the comfort that is received as a result of the mourning.

Read Isaiah 61:1-3, which refers to the coming of Jesus. According these verses, what will Jesus give to those who mourn?

___

Turn to James 4:7-10 and read through it a couple of times. Once you are finished, answer the following questions.

What is our attitude toward sin to be?

___

___

What do you see in our world today concerning sin?

___

___

Look around us today. What is the world's attitude toward sin? Is it not an attitude of complacency and acceptance? Beloved, we are to mourn over sin in the world. Our hearts are to break over it and, God forbid, we are never to laugh at it. How can we laugh over sin, beloved, when sin nailed Jesus to the cross?

Jeremiah is referred to as the weeping prophet because he was a man who deeply mourned over the sin of God's people. Read the passages taken from Jeremiah 8 and 9 and answer the questions that follow. I believe it gives a beautiful picture of the heart of God and what He feels toward sin.

Jeremiah 8:18-22

[18]My sorrow is beyond healing, My heart is faint within me!
[19]Behold listen! The cry of the daughter of my people from a distant land: "Is the Lord not in Zion? Is her King not within her?" "Why have they provoked me with their graven images, with foreign idol?"

²⁰ *"Harvest is past, summer is ended, and we are not saved."*
²¹ *For the brokenness of the daughter of my people I am broken; I mourn, dismay has taken hold of me.*
²² *Is there no balm in Gilead? Is there no physician there? Why then has not the health of the daughter of my people been restored?*

Jeremiah 9:1 & 17-20

¹ *Oh that my head were waters and my eyes a fountain of tears, that I might weep day and night for the slain of the daughter of my people!*
¹⁷ *Thus says the Lord of hosts, "Consider and call for the mourning women, that they may come; And send for the wailing women, that they may come!*
¹⁸ *"Let them make haste and take up a wailing for us, that our eyes may shed tears and our eyelids flow with water.*
¹⁹ *"For a voice of wailing is heard from Zion, 'How are we ruined! We areput to great shame, for we have left the land, because they have cast down our dwellings.'"*
²⁰ *Now hear the word of the Lord, O you women, and let your ear receive the word of His mouth; teach your daughters wailing, and everyone her neighbor a dirge.*

What was Jeremiah's attitude toward the sin of others?

_____

Did Jeremiah weep over the sin of the people?

_____

Let's read through these verses once more, but this time I want you to draw a box around every reference to wailing or mourning. Use the color of your choice!

From your markings, what did you learn about wailing or mourning?

Wailing / Mourning

_____

_____

_____

What kind of women was God calling for?

_____

What were they to do because of sin?

_____

Why were they to take up a wailing?

_____

Who were they to teach this to?

_____

God's desire, beloved, is for every generation to weep and mourn over sin. Sin breaks the very heart of God and it should break our hearts as well. The sin of the world brought death because the wages of sin is death (Romans 8:23). Sin brought death to Jesus, God's only son. So we learn that we are not only to mourn over sin in our life and sin in the Church, but we are to mourn over sin in the world. Knowing these three truths, let's list them out below.

The Three Things We Are to Mourn Over

1. _____

2. _____

3. _____

Knowing these, beloved, brings us to our final principle in this week's study. It is…

Principle
We are to mourn over all sin

There is no sin that we are not to mourn over. All sin should break our hearts because it breaks the very heart of God. When we mourn over sin, God not only sees this but the world sees it as well. We are the heart of God to the world and it gives them the opportunity to join in with us in mourning over sin. Do you remember the wonderful benefit of mourning according to Jesus?

Write it out below just so you see it once more. I've started it for you.

"Blessed are those who _____, for they shall be _____."

Turn to your Word Windows Section and find the meaning for **"comfort"** as used here in Matthew 5.

Comfort

_____

_____

Wow! What a word! Do you see, precious student? When we mourn over sin, God will draw us up to His loving side and he will console us. There is no comfort like the comfort of God. There is no peace like being drawn up into the hands of Jehovah. It is in this comforting that we learn of His all-sufficient breast, where we learn intimacy with the Father. It is here in these moments of intimacy, oh daughter, that your heart begins to beat as one with your Father's heart.

This is the powerful benefit of Godly mourning. When we mourn over sin…

Benefit
God will comfort us

What a loving, merciful Father we have. This is when this beatitude begins to make sense to us. How can a person who mourns be happy? It doesn't make sense from the outward appearance, does it? When we delve into it we see that mourning brings the comfort of God. To know the comfort of God in the midst of Godly sorrow will bring true joy into the heart and life of the mourner. It will bring a joy that they would never have experienced in any other way.

Turn to The Blessed Life Chart in the back of the book and write in the second Beatitude. Once you've finished, write out our memory verse for the week in the space provided. Try to write it out without looking. You want to make sure you have fully committed it to memory and this will tell the tale! Write the scripture reference also.

Memory Verse

_____

_____

Now, let's take minute to review our principles and benefits for this week.

Week in Review

Principle # 1: *Mourning finds its birthplace in the heart of God*
Benefit: *A Pattern for mourning is given*

Principle # 2: *Sin mars life*
Benefit: *The Glory of God is hidden*

Principle #3: *God is not honored when sin is present*
Benefit: *God is not in His proper place*

Principle #4: *We are to mourn over all sin*
Benefit: *God will comfort us*

Personal Evaluation

When was the last time you mourned over sin?

Is there sin in your life that you have not repented of?

Do you pray that God will cause your heart to beat as one with His?

Well, beloved student, you have worked so very hard this week. Thank you for hanging in there and for working so diligently. I'm so proud of you. The truths that we've learned have not been easy but they are necessary. I will leave you with a final thought:

What will you do with the truth that God gives you?

I will see you in our lesson time together. Much love to you!

Pam

LESSON THREE
The Gentle, the Hungry and the Thirsty

Day One

Israel had waited for hundreds of years for their Messiah to come that He might save them from their oppressors. They thought that their Savior would come as a powerful and mighty warrior, but instead He came meek and mild as a sheep to the slaughter. Because He came in a way that they did not expect, they missed the very Lamb of God as He sat before them speaking such wonderful truths on a hillside long ago. What kind of mighty warrior would come to rescue His people saying things like: *"Blessed are those who mourn, blessed are those who are poor in spirit, and those who are persecuted?"*

This was not at all what they expected. The problem was not with Jesus' teaching but rather with the people and their preconceived ideas about their expected Savior. You see, the people had an idea of what they thought Jesus should be like and what He should do and because He didn't fit their mold, they refused to accept Him. It is much this way still today, beloved student. May I ask you a question? What do you think Jesus is like or what do you think He may have been like when He walked this earth? I believe most of us would agree that He was probably a gentle man, but would He have been hungry and thirsty? And if so, what would He have hungered or thirsted for? Would God's only son, the Savior of the lost world be in need of anything? Would He have experienced pain or discomfort? Would the Savior of the world willingly subject Himself to the hands of man? These are all questions to consider beloved.

This week as we look a little deeper into Jesus' Sermon on the Mount, we will look at Jesus' call to gentleness and we will learn the deep secrets of how to be truly satisfied. Beloved, it may not be what you expect. Remember to pray before you begin and ask God to reveal truth to your inner most being.

Today let's begin our study time together by reading through Matthew Chapters 5, 6 & 7. Remember, repetition provides for fruitful study. By the time we are through with this study you will know the Sermon on the Mount as you have never known it before. Once you have read through the passage, I want us to look at the next "blessed" or "beatitude" that Jesus gives us. To help us get started, let's write out Matthew 5:5 together in the space provided.

• **Matthew 5:5**

_____

_____

_____

Turn to your Word Windows section and look up the definition for the word "gentle" as used in this verse. If you are using the King James Version this verse will read: *"Blessed are the meek."* Once you've found the definition for the word **"gentle",** write it out in the space provided.

Gentle/Meek

_____

_____

Based on the meaning of this word, would you say that the kind of gentleness or meekness that Jesus' is referring to in Matthew 5:5 is a way of life or just a characteristic that shows itself only in certain circumstances?

_____

_____

Look up Matthew 11:28-30 and read it carefully. Based on these verses could, we say that Jesus was gentle or (meek)?

_____

_____

Let's look at one more passage. Turn to Matthew Chapter 21 and read Verses 1-14. How is Jesus described in Verse 5?

_____

_____

How would you describe Jesus in Verses 12 & 13?

_____

_____

Jesus was described as gentle but yet we see him turning over the tables of the money changers and even driving them out of the temple. This is quite a contrast from when He rode into the city of Jerusalem isn't it beloved? He came in gentleness but yet He displayed anger. How can this be? Gentleness is often equated with weakness, the presence of fear, and even the absence of conviction. Meekness or gentleness has often been defined as anger that is under control. Meekness is never apathetic.

Some believe that being angry is a sin and cannot be an acceptable behavior for a Christian or especially someone who is described as being gentle or meek.

If this were true then Jesus would have been in sin when He entered the temple that day and drove out the merchants turning over their tables. Since Jesus was the spotless or sinless Lamb of God, this cannot be true. Would you say that a gentle person can display anger over something and still be considered gentle or meek? To help us understand this a little better, let's see what God tells us by looking up and writing down Ephesians 4:26 in the space below.

- **Ephesians 4:26**

_____

_____

_____

According to this verse, can a person be angry and not be in sin? Explain your answer.

_____

_____

You see, beloved, there are many facets to meekness or gentleness. True meekness will always display humble submission to God, to His way, to His will and will never contend with God. This is where confusion often comes in when trying to understand what true meekness is in the eyes of God and in the life of one of His children. To help us take a deeper look and gain a better understanding of this word 'meekness,' let's look together at Psalm 37. It will be our main passage of study as we look at meekness together. It is typed out for you at the end of this week's lesson. After you locate it, read through it once and then we will begin to dig into this wonderful Psalm that sheds so much light on the lifestyle of the meek.

Now that you've read through this chapter of Psalms, go back through it again, this time marking every reference to the wicked who are also referred to as evildoers or wrongdoers. Draw a rectangle around every reference to these and all their pronouns as well. Use the color of your choice, beloved, as long as it will stand out to you when you go back through the text. Once you have finished, go back to every place you marked and make a list of what you learned about the wicked. Take your time, making sure you don't miss any. This will be a most valuable learning time if you don't rush it. There is much to learn in this wonderful Psalm. Inductive Bible Study takes time and patience, just like the farmer who plows and plants his seeds often waiting for weeks before he sees any sign of life. It is the same when gleaning fruit from God's Word giving a great reward for those who are diligent and steadfast, waiting patiently for the harvest. So with that in mind, let's get started.

The Wicked /Evildoers/Wrongdoers

What do the wicked do or try to do to the righteous?

_____

_____

Based on what you learned, what is the future of the wicked?

_____

_____

Does the Lord know about the wicked and the things they do? Can they hide their deeds from God?

_____

_____

Does God know when the wicked come against the righteous? If so, how does God respond when He sees this?

_____

_____

Our behavior is often affected by the behavior of others. When we look closely at this Psalm, we find that we are not to concern ourselves with the wicked or with evil or wrongdoers. Isn't it comforting to know that God is not at all concerned with the wicked or when they scheme or come against His own? What should that mean to us as God's children?

_____

To help us better understand this let's read through Psalm 37 once more, but this time I want you to draw a purple triangle around every reference to God making sure you get all the pronouns as well. Once you're finished, list everything you learned about God from marking the text in the space provided. Remember, truth is revealed little by little and it takes time. There is no substitute for Inductive Bible Study when it is done slowly and methodically. In doing this, beloved, you are learning more about your God and as you come to know Him more, you will love Him more and you will trust Him more. We could spend an eternity drinking the eternal fountain of the knowledge of God and never be able to drink our fill. So as you make your list, drink in God and all that you learn He is for He satisfies the thirsty soul as none other.

GOD

_____

_____

_____

_____

_____

_____

Based on what you learned about God, beloved what kind of heart does He have toward the righteous? Is He for the righteous? Explain your answer.

_____

_____

This is where meekness finds its birthplace, beloved, in knowing that God's heart is set upon the righteous and it is set against the wicked. The meek understand that it is not their place to deal with the wicked. It is God's place and it is His promise to us that He will deal with them in His time and in His way. The heart of meekness beats this one truth over and over again....

Principle
God rules over the righteous and the wicked

When we understand that God is fully aware of the activity and intents of the wicked, we can also know that their deeds will not go unpunished and this should bring our hearts comfort. Three times in Psalm 37 the righteous are told not to fret. See if you can find all three and once you do, underline them with the color of your choice.

According to these three places, why are we not to fret over evildoers or the wicked? What will it lead to?

_____

_____

Look up the word **"fret"** in your Word Windows Section and write out its meaning in the space provided for you.

Fret

_____

_____

Think with me for a moment. Why do we usually fret over evildoers?

_____

_____

We are not to fret because God knows and He will act on behalf of all those who belong to Him. God never intended for the righteous to deal with the wicked because that is His place and His promise to us that He will. The wicked will not go unpunished because God is not blind. He is a holy and just God. He is the avenger of the righteous, beloved, because they are His and He is committed to protecting and preserving them until the very end. He is God over the righteous and the unrighteous, for He rules over all and there is none above Him. When the righteous understand and believe that God rules over the righteous and the wicked then…

Benefit
Anger is controlled

This is where righteous anger comes in. It's anger over the sin while bowing the knee before the One who will deal with all sin. Meekness will always rest in quiet submission before the throne of God. Meekness is a quiet strength that draws its courage from the knowledge that God is the rightful avenger. Meekness will never cower in fear and will never take matters into its own hands because these things have never left the hands of God. This is why meekness is one of the most powerful tools of witness in the lives of believers. Meekness is power drawn from the truth of God's sovereignty. The most powerful strength of all is that strength that is never heard, only seen. Quiet strength is a rare find and when it is found it is often misunderstood or mistaken for apathy. I heard a true story once that I believe gives a beautiful picture of meekness.

There once was a hard working farmer who set out to plant a garden so he and his family would have food for the winter. He carefully chose the perfect spot where just the right amount of sunshine would fall and he began to clear away all the stones and till up the hard ground. Day after day the hard working farmer labored tirelessly, clearing his precious field until it was finally ready for planting. He planted his seed with much care throughout each row and watered them thoroughly in hopes of a grand harvest. How proud the hard working farmer was when he began to see the tiny shoots of life spring up through the fertile soil. He lovingly tended to his garden each day, pulling weeds and hoeing around every plant.

Finally, the day of harvest had come. The hardworking farmer woke up with great anticipation of gathering his beloved harvest as he headed toward the field. Much to his surprise he found that someone had beat him to the harvest and there was nothing left on the vines for he and his family. He quickly went next door to his neighbor's house and asked if he had seen anything. His neighbor was quick to tell the hard working farmer that he was the one who came and took his harvest in the night. The hard working farmer stood there, bewildered, but was finally able to ask his neighbor, "Why would you do such a thing?". The neighbor, showing no remorse for what he had done, answered, "because I wanted to and I need food for the winter also". The hard working farmer told his neighbor to keep what he had taken but to please not go into his garden in the future, for he and his family really needed the food for the winter, also. The neighbor only laughed at the farmer, telling him that he would keep coming back until he had taken all that he wanted.

The hard working farmer sought the Lord that night in prayer asking Him what he should do and also pleading with the Lord to punish the wicked neighbor. He just could not understand how anyone could be so wicked and not be punished for such a horrible deed. After a long night seeking the Lord, the hardworking farmer emerged the next morning with the answer the Lord had given him. He took his horse and plow and headed to his neighbor's land. He looked around his neighbor's property until he found the perfect spot and then began clearing away the stones. He worked diligently all day until the field was cleared and he could begin plowing. His neighbor came out in utter shock as he saw the farmer working his land. He asked him what was he doing. The hard working farmer replied: "The Lord told me in the night to see to your neighbor's needs first and then He will see to mine."

This is meekness, beloved; quiet strength characterized by controlled anger. How powerful and humbling this story is. A yielded spirit is a precious jewel in the hands of the sovereign God.

One more thing before we go. As you know we are learning a new verse every week by committing it to memory. This week's verse is typed out for you below. Read through it several times and then we will call it a day.

Psalm 22:5

"To you they cried out and were delivered; in you they trusted and were not disappointed."

Well, precious student, you've worked very hard today. If I could come along side of you right now, I would put my arms around you and hug you tightly, telling you how proud I am of you for being diligent to study God's Word and for hungering to know Him more. Thank you for staying the course thus far. Rest for now and meditate on all that you've learned today, asking God to help you soak it up into the deep places of your heart.

I will see you on Day Two.

Day Two

On Day One of this week we began looking into the life of one who is gentle or meek. We saw that meekness is a quiet strength, that it is anger under control. Today, we want to continue studying this Beatitude and the wonderful promise given by Jesus to those who live a life of meekness. Pray before you begin, beloved, and ask the Lord to reveal truth to you today as you study His precious Word, then meet me back here.

Turn to the back of this week's lesson and locate Psalm 37 that is typed out for you. As we saw yesterday in our time of study, this Psalm speaks about the wicked and the righteous and what will happen to them in the end. Today, we want to look at the righteous. Let's begin by reading through the Psalm to re-familiarize ourselves with this passage. Once you're finished, read through it a second time, but this time as you go through it, I want you to mark every reference to the righteous by drawing a circle around each with the color of your choice. Just make sure it is a different color than you used for the other markings you've done thus far.

Make a list in the space provided of everything you learned about the righteous from marking the text.

The Righteous

_____

_____

_____

_____

_____

Turn back to Matthew 5:5 and write out this Beatitude once more in the space provided, I have started it for you.

"Blessed are the _____ for they shall _____.

According to this verse, what will the meek inherit?

_____

There is a wonderful promise made to those who are meek! The Lord said that the meek will inherit the earth. What a magnificent promise, beloved. Let's read through our text once more, but this time as you go through it I want you to mark every place the word "inherit" or "inheritance" is used. 'Inherit 'or 'inheritance' are key words used in this Psalm and it is vital to understanding meekness. There are six places that these words are used. Try find all six of them.

Based on your markings, what did you learn about the inheritance of the righteous or the humble (same meaning as meek)?

_____

_____

_____

From what we've seen so far, beloved, we know that the righteous or the meek, will inherit the earth. But exactly what does that mean to us? How can we inherit the earth? To help us better understand what Jesus was saying when He spoke these words in Matthew 5:5, let's turn to our Word Windows Section and look up the meaning of the word "**Inherit**" or "**Inheritance**". Once you've located it write it out in the space provided for you.

Inherit

_____

_____

_____

Based on the meaning of this word "inherit", what do you think it means to "inherit the earth?" Think about your answer for a few minutes and remember, there are no wrong or right answers.

_____

_____

_____

If we were to take this meaning of "inherit" and put it in our Beatitude it would read something like this: *Blessed are the meek because they will occupy, and overcome without fail in the land that God gives them by driving out those who occupy it.*

I believe a perfect example of this is found in the life of Joseph, the son of Jacob, grandson of Isaac, great grandson of Abraham. Let's turn to and read Genesis Chapter 45 and Chapter 50. Before you read these two chapters, let me put you into the right time frame and what had happened so you will understand the events that are taking place. Joseph was sold into slavery by his other brothers when he was very young. While Joseph was enslaved, he endured a lot of things, but God elevated Him in the house of Pharaoh, giving him much favor.

God had given Joseph a very special gift of interpreting dreams. Pharaoh had a dream that no one could interpret so after hearing about Joseph, he sent for him to come and interpret a most disturbing dream that he had. Joseph explained the meaning of the dream to Pharaoh by telling him that a great famine was coming to the land and that they should prepare for it so the people would not starve. Because of Joseph's ability to interpret his dream, Pharaoh exalted Joseph to second in command in all the land of Egypt. Sure enough, the famine came and the entire country was without food including the land of Canaan where Joseph's family lived. Jacob sent his sons into the land of Egypt because they had heard that the land of Egypt had storehouses of food. Jacob's brothers had already come once to see Joseph and now, in Chapter 45 of Genesis, they had returned with their youngest brother, Benjamin, Joseph had requested them. At this point in the story, they still had no idea that Joseph was their long lost brother. This is where we will begin our story. Read through these two chapters, or if you like, read all the chapters between 45 and 50. It's a wonderful story of God's preservation of life.

Once you've read through these chapters, meet me back here to answers some questions about what you've read.

What was Joseph's attitude toward what had happened? Was he bitter or angry with his brothers? Was he seeking any kind of revenge?

_____

_____

Why do you think Joseph had the attitude that he did?

_____

_____

The most powerful verses describing the life of Joseph are found in Genesis 45:5-8 and 50:19-21. I have typed these out for you. Take a minute and read over these verses.

Genesis 45:5-8

⁵"Now do not be grieved or angry with yourselves, because you sold me here, for God sent me before you to preserve life.

⁶"For the famine has been in the land these two years, and there are still five years in which there will be neither plowing nor harvesting

⁷"God sent me before you to preserve for you a remnant in the earth, and to keep you alive by a great deliverance.

⁸"Now, therefore, it was not you who sent me here, but God: and He has made me a father to Pharaoh and lord of all his household and ruler over all the land of Egypt.

Genesis 50:19-21

[19] But Joseph said to them, "Do not be afraid, for am I in God's place? *[20] "As for you, you meant evil against me, but God meant it for good in order to bring about this present result, to preserve many people alive.* *[21] "So therefore, do not be afraid; I will provide for you and your little ones." So he comforted them and spoke kindly to them.*

What was Joseph's attitude toward his situation and what had happened to him?

_____

_____

What was Joseph's attitude toward his brothers?

_____

_____

One last question: What was Joseph's attitude toward God?

_____

_____

As you can see, beloved, this is a story of true meekness. Although Joseph was sold into slavery by his own brothers, betrayed and taken away from his parents and the only home he had ever known, he still offered comfort and consolation to his brothers. If anyone had the right to be bitter or even to take revenge with his brothers for the wrong they had done, it was Joseph. Joseph had the power to have them all put to death with just a spoken word. But rather than being angry or vengeful, we see a man who accepted what had happened to him. What made the difference, beloved? How can someone who endured what Joseph did respond in such a manner? Instead of being angry with them,

THE BLESSED WOMAN

he consoled them; he gave them reassurance and even promised to take care of them and their families. That's unheard of today!

Do you see the parallel, beloved student? Remember our meaning for meekness; that it is anger under control because it recognizes that God rules over all. Joseph recognized the hand of God in his life and that God had a purpose for it all. This is where meekness finds its strength: in knowing that God has a purpose in everything. Meekness understands that all things work together for good to those who love God and are called according to His purpose (Romans 8:28).

Do you remember what the benefit of meekness is? What promise did Jesus give to His listener that day? See if you can finish the verse.

"Blessed are the meek, for they shall _____."

In the light of this promise and in the light of the word study we did on "inherit," do you think Joseph inherited the earth? Did he receive the promise that accompanies meekness? Explain your answer.

_____

_____

Meekness has a great promise, beloved. It is the promise to all those who entrust themselves into the hands of a sovereign God that they will regain lost ground in their lives. What did Joseph lose? Think about all that he lost before you answer.

_____

_____

Was any of this given back to him? If so, what and how?

_____

_____

What a powerful principle we learn about meekness or gentleness from the life of Joseph.

Principle
Meekness looks through the eyes of Sovereignty

Understanding God's perspective is usually not the difficult part for us but rather it's accepting it. Joseph saw God's perspective in time and he embraced it because He knew God had a higher purpose and that was to preserve life. It's living for something greater than yourself. Joseph made a very powerful statement in Genesis 50:19 where he said, *"I am in God's place."* Let these words sink down into your heart and settle there for just a moment. This statement, this verse reveals the true heart of meekness. Meekness always looks through the eyes of God's sovereignty. To help us fully understand this concept let's turn to our Word Windows Section and find the meaning of the word "**Place**". Once you've located it, write down the meaning in the space provided for you.

Place

_____

_____

Based on the meaning of the word "place", what do you think Joseph meant when he said: *"I am in God's place."*

_____

_____

I believe that Joseph recognized that the things that occur in our lives that bring us low, those things that humble us, are ordained of God. There are places that God ordained for you to occupy long before you were ever born. These are places that will bring us low so that God may raise us up just as he did Joseph. Higher ground begins in the low places, beloved, and to get to the mountaintop one must first pass through the valleys below.

There is a powerful verse that says this so beautifully. Look up Psalm 18:35 and write it out in the space provided. I believe it will bless your soul as it has mine!

- **Psalm 18:35**

_____

_____

_____

Did you catch that powerful truth? *"Thy gentleness makes me great!"* Greatness is found in gentleness (meekness). Do you recognize God's place beloved daughter? Meekness embraces those places ordained by God because meekness looks through the eyes of sovereignty and when this happens, beloved….

Benefit
The soul is at perfect peace

There is only place that the soul of man can find peace and that is when it finds itself in the place where God has placed it. God's ways are not our ways and His thoughts are not our thoughts. But His way is always perfect, beloved, and He is always bringing about good and not evil. This is why Joseph could put his arms around the very ones who did evil to him and tell them not to be afraid that he meant them no harm. There was no bitterness in Joseph's heart, no malice, no blaming, and most of all, no regrets. Joseph never said, "I wish this had never happened." How powerful is the life that is fully surrendered into the hands of God. What a testimony to his brothers and to the Pharaoh who knew what had been done to Joseph. The greater the suffering, the greater the ministry.

Is your soul restless? Is it looking for peace? Do you find yourself in a place where you are contending with God? Are you questioning why? What have you learned through today's study that might help you or someone else who may be struggling?

_____

_____

_____

_____

God's place for Joseph involved betrayal, loneliness, sadness, suffering, forgiveness and submission but in the end it brought life. Through the death of Joseph's old life, life was given to thousands and death was conquered. The place of God will often make no sense to the human mind, but in the end it will be found to be most perfect. It is there in those God places we find life-giving springs that only flow from the depths of sorrow. This is when we find that the light of God is as deep as the shadows. Meekness holds itself steady even in the darkest hour because it knows that day will break forth over the horizon bringing with it the glory of God. Meekness concerns itself with one thing beloved daughter: *To trust God in all things.*

What powerful truths God has revealed to us today. I have prayed that when you reach this part of the study, you will embrace truth and see truth as you have never seen it before. The life that embraces the truths of God will never be the same.

Take a moment and turn to the back of your study book until you come the to "The Blessed Life" chart. Once you've found it, write down this blessedness on meekness. Remember, we are building a chart of truth for that life that is truly blessed, the life that has found true happiness. You will have a goldmine of truth by the time we are finished.

Let's close our time together by reviewing this week's memory verse. Take a few minutes to read over it before you put your book away. Thank you for working so hard today, beloved. These truths are not easy ones but they are God's.

Much love to you, precious student. I will see you on Day Three.

THE BLESSED WOMAN

Day Three

    If you could look into the deep places of your heart you would find hidden there your greatest fears, your dreams, your plans for the future and even your regrets from the past. Our heart is the very storehouse of everything about our life, good and bad and everything that we hope it will be. The psalmist said, "out of the heart flow the issues of life." Our heart will give us away every time, beloved, for it cannot hide what's inside. If I were to ask you what is the desire of your heart, what would you say? Some people spend their whole lives chasing after the dreams that are within their hearts. The heart is what turns us, what stops us or motivates us to certain actions. The heart is what will cause us to give up living all together or to choose to live life to its fullest every day. The heart is what God looks at, beloved, for He fashioned it to be the most powerful tool in the life of His creation. Psalm 84:5 says: *"How blessed is the man whose strength is in You, in whose heart are the highways to Zion!"* May our hearts, beloved, show the world the way to God.

    Today we will journey into the very heart of man. Pray before you begin, asking God to reveal truth to your mind and to your heart. Let's begin by reacquainting ourselves with Matthew Chapters 5, 6 and 7 by reading through these chapters.

    What "Blessed" does Jesus give in Matthew 5:6? After locating this verse, fill in the blanks in the space provided.

"Blessed are those who _____

for _____ *for they shall be* _____."

    This is our next "Blessed" that we will study during our next two days of this week's study. According to this verse, what did Jesus say that the blessed person would hunger and thirst for?

_____

To help us understand this thirst and this hunger, let's turn to our Word Windows Section and look up the meaning of these two words. Once you've found them, write them in the space provided for you.

Hunger

_____

_____

Thirst

_____

_____

Based on the meaning of these two words, what do you think it means to hunger and thirst?

_____

_____

Look up the following verses and write down what you learn about the one who is thirsty, or the one who yearns or seeks. Note what they are desiring and why.

- **Psalm 42:1**

_____

_____

_____

- **Psalm 63:1**

- **Psalm 84:2**

- **Zephaniah 2:3**

We know that those who are "blessed" will hunger and thirst for righteousness. But what does this mean to us as God's children? I believe it will help shed some light on this beatitude if we look up the meaning of "**righteousness**" in our Word Windows Section. You have looked up this word previously in week one of our study. It is the same word so, for the sake of review and new insight let's revisit this word meaning. Once you've found it write down the meaning in the space provided.

Righteousness

_____

_____

I want you think with me for a moment, beloved. How would you describe righteousness? What would righteousness look like if it were lived out? In other words, what are some characteristics of righteousness or a righteous person.? How would you know righteousness if you saw it? Meditate on this for a moment then list your thoughts in the space provided.

Righteousness

_____

_____

_____

_____

_____

It's always good to revisit your birthplace, beloved. I have typed out for you Genesis 1:26-28a. These verses give us a look into the heart of God and why He created man and woman. Take a moment and read over these verses and then answer the questions that follow.

Genesis 1:26-28a

"Then God said, 'Let Us make man in Our image, according to Our likeness; and let them rule over the fish of the sea and over the birds of the sky and over the cattle and over all the earth and over every creeping thing that creeps on the earth.' God created man in His own image, and

in the image of God He created him; male and female He created them. God blessed them..."

Why did God make man and woman?

_____

_____

What pattern did God use to make man and woman?

_____

_____

According to this passage, what kind of woman were you created to be?

_____

_____

Did you know that you and I were birthed in the heart of God long before we were birthed on the earth? When God created us, He created us in His image, in the likeness of Himself. In other words, God wanted the world to be able to see Him in us! We are to mirror our Holy God, our loving and gracious Heavenly Father. We are to be like God, beloved! Righteousness is being right with God so we can be like God in all things. If we are not right with God, then we cannot be like Him and if we are not like Him, then how will the world ever come to know Him? God's desire is for the world to know Him and His son through us, His children. And so when God created us in His likeness, He put within us the need to be like Him. With this thought, beloved, comes a powerful principle...

Principle
We are to crave to be like God

This is why Jesus said that the person who is truly blessed will hunger and thirst for righteousness, because we were created for that purpose. When we find our purpose for living then we truly can begin to live. What do you crave the most? What do you desire more than any other thing? Another way that may help you answer this is to think about your greatest fears, your deepest concerns in life. If you could take a moment to think over these things and list them. What would be at the top of that list? Would you be willing to do that right now, beloved? Would you be willing to be gut level honest? Take a moment and make your list on a separate sheet of paper and then take note of what was at the top of your list.

What was at the top of your list, daughter? What is the thing that you desire the most? What is your greatest concern or fear?

_____

_____

Was your greatest concern being what God wanted you to be? Was your heart's desire above all to be pleasing to God? Is your biggest fear to have the world look at you and not see God? Oh, if this were true of all us! Whatever it is that you wrote down or didn't write down but chose to store it in your heart, God knows what it is. He sees that and He understands your struggles and your deepest concerns. Jesus made it clear that day up on a hillside that we are to hunger and thirst to be like God, to be like Him. And when we crave to be like God, something miraculous happens…

Benefit
Our purpose for living is found

Do you remember that our meaning for 'righteousness' is to be just or right? With that in mind, I have typed out Micah 6:8 for you to read.

Micah 6:8

"He has told you, oh man, what is good; and what does the Lord require of you but to do justice, to love kindness, and to walk humbly with your God?"

What does the Lord require of you, beloved?

_____

_____

The Lord wants our greatest desire to be to yearn to be like Him more than life itself. This is His heart's requirement of us, daughter. God wants to be your treasure. He wants to be the apple of your eye. When we wake every morning, may our cry be, *"Oh Lord all I want is more of You"*. May it be said of us! Why don't you take time right now and find a quiet place to get alone with God. Ask Him to search your heart and burn every desire away except the desire for Him. The eyes of God roam to and fro over the entire Earth searching and trying the heart of each of us. When He finds the heart that is fully His, then God rejoices and He reaches out and grabs hold of that heart that He may strongly support it (II Chronicles 16:9).

As we come to a close today take time and review your memory verse by reading over several times. Thank you for studying God's Word. I am ever so proud of you. I will see you on Day Four as we close out this week together.

Day Four

Welcome back, beloved student. I have been so excited for you to begin today's study! Have you ever met, or do you know, a person who is never satisfied? A person that no matter what you do for them or what is given to them, they are never content? Believe it or not, this describes the majority of the people in the world today. In fact, it is a rarity to find a person who is truly satisfied with their life. A person who can survey their life and conclude that they want nothing else because they are completely satisfied. Most people might say that it is impossible to have a life like that. Yet Jesus, in His Sermon on the Mount, told His listeners over two thousand years ago that all those who hunger and thirst for righteousness would be satisfied. This is one of the best kept secrets of the world beloved! We know how we can be truly satisfied. It is possible. There is hope. These words were coming from the One Who was Life Himself. As you remember from yesterday's lesson, we saw from God's Word that we are to crave to be like God because this is why we were created.

Today, we are going to look at the promise that Jesus made to all those who hunger and thirst for righteousness. What a promise it is! I love that about God. He not only gives us these wonderful truths, but with them come wonderful promises! What a gracious giving God we have. He doesn't have to give us a thing, beloved, but He lavishes His promises upon us through the truths of His Word. This is going to be an awesome study today, so hang on. Take time to pray and seek the Lord, asking Him for Godly wisdom as you study His Word today.

To help us get started, beloved, write out the "blessed" that we began studying on day three of this week that is found in Matthew 5:6. I have filled in some of it for you already.

"Blessed are those who _____ and _____ for _____ for they shall be _____."

According to Jesus' Words, what will happen to all those who hunger and thirst for righteousness?

_____

Turn to your Word Windows Section and locate the meaning for the word **"Satisfied"** as used here in Matthew 5:6 and write it out in the space provided for you. The word for **"Satisfied"** in the King James Version is 'filled.'

Satisfied *(KJV—filled)*

_____

_____

THE BLESSED WOMAN

Based on the meaning of this word, would a person who is 'satisfied' be in need of anything? Explain your answer.

_____

_____

Below you will find Psalm 81:10-16 typed out for you. Take time to read it through once before we study it together.

Psalm 81:10-16

¹⁰I, the Lord, am your God, who brought you up from the land of Egypt; Open your mouth wide and I will fill it.
¹¹But My people did not listen to My voice, and Israel did not obey Me.
¹²So I gave them over to the stubbornness of their heart, to walk in their own devices.
¹³"Oh that My people would listen to me, that Israel would walk in My ways!
¹⁴"I would quickly subdue their enemies and turn My hand against their adversaries.
¹⁵"Those who hate the Lord would pretend obedience to Him, and their time of punishment would be forever.
¹⁶But I would feed you with the finest of wheat, and with honey from the rock I would satisfy you."

Now that you've read through this passage, I want you to go back through it again but this time as you do, draw a purple triangle around every reference to God. Once you've finished, list the things that you learned about God from marking the text. Make sure you get all the pronouns that refer to God as well.

God

According to verses 10 and 16, what is God's desire for His people? What does He want to do for them?

Look up the following verses and note what you learn from each concerning the life that is satisfied.

- **Psalm 17:15**

- **Psalm 145:14-16**

- **Psalm 65:4**

_____

_____

_____

One more, beloved, and we will be through. I want you to soak in these next verses.

- **Psalm 73:25-26** (these are some of my favorite verses!)

_____

_____

_____

Do you see it, beloved? The heart that desires nothing on earth, but only God who is in heaven, will have God as their portion! God will be their all in all. The heart that yearns after God will have no regrets. God is the only one that can satisfy! When we desire to be like Him, He promises to satisfy us and fill us to overflowing. There is no greater comfort than these words. These must have been such foreign words to the crowd listening to Jesus that day. With these verses precious student, we find a powerful Principle…

Principle
Only God can satisfy

Have you drawn from other wells, beloved, looking for true satisfaction in all the wrong places only to come up empty? Jesus told His listeners that day that there was a place, a life that would have no regrets, no wants, no changes except for more of the living God. It is that life that will say: "Just give me Jesus." He is all I want and He is all I will ever need. Is this your heart's cry, beloved? It's purposing in your heart to say to the Lord every moment of every day: *"My heart belongs to you, oh Lord, and I will not give myself to another."*

There is a Psalm full of this powerful truth that I want you to take time to read. It is Psalm 91. There are 16 verses and as you read through them, I want you to take note of the life of the one who loves the Lord, the one who seeks Him. These are such comforting words and they help reconfirm all that we've learned. Write down what you note about this person in the space provided.

- **Psalm 91:1-16**

_____

_____

_____

When we find that God is the only one who can satisfy then...

Benefit
There are no regrets

You will have no regrets, beloved, if you will live a life that yearns for God. A life that craves to be like the living God. He says to us: *"Open thy mouth wide and I will fill it."* God keeps His promises and He will fill the mouth of the thirsty. Praise His Holy name. Well, beloved, we have come to the end of the week. Let's review what we've learned this week. Turn to The Blessed Life Chart and fill in this fourth Beatitude and then read through the week in review.

Week in Review

Principle # 1: *God rules over the righteous and the wicked*
Benefit: *Anger is controlled*

Principle # 2: *Meekness looks through the eyes of sovereignty*
Benefit: *The soul is at perfect peace*

Principle #3: *We are to crave to be like God*
Benefit: *Our purpose for living is found*

Principle #4: *Only God can satisfy*
Benefit: *There are no regrets*

As we close out our time together this week, let me leave you with these questions for you to ponder as you go before the Lord. As you read through these, don't read in haste, but rather ask yourself what your answer would be. Ask God to search your heart to see if there is any hurtful way or anything there that should not be.

Personal Evaluation

Are you striving with God over the place that He has you in, beloved?

Do you have anger that is out of control?

Do you yearn to be like God?

When people look at you, can they see Jesus?

Is God first in your life, or have you given your heart to another?

Well, beloved, we have come to the end of our third week together. I know I've left you with some difficult questions. This has not been an easy week of study because of the hard truths we've studied. I have paused here at this place and I have prayed for you, precious student. Though I may never see your face, I have prayed that your face would be the reflection of the One who created you. The day you were born, God Himself bent down and breathed life into you because He wanted His face to be the first thing that your eyes would see. God set His heart upon you beloved. Will you set your heart upon Him?

Much love to you, daughter. I will see you in our lesson time together.

Psalm 37

¹Do not fret because of evildoers, be not envious toward wrongdoers.
²For they will wither quickly like the grass and fade like the green herb.
³Trust in the LORD and do good; Dwell in the land and cultivate faithfulness.
⁴Delight yourself in the LORD; And He will give you the desires of your heart.
⁵Commit your way to the LORD, trust also in Him, and He will do it.
⁶He will bring forth your righteousness as the light and your judgment as the noonday.
⁷Rest in the LORD and wait patiently for Him; Do not fret because of him who prospers in his way, because of the man who carries out wicked schemes.
⁸Cease from anger and forsake wrath; Do not fret, it leads only to evildoing.
⁹For evildoers will be cut off, but those who wait for the LORD, they will inherit the land.
¹⁰Yet a little while and the wicked man will be no more; And you will look carefully for his place and he will not be there.
¹¹But the humble will inherit the land and will delight themselves in abundant prosperity.
¹²The wicked plots against the righteous and gnashes at him with his teeth.
¹³The LORD laughs at him, for He sees his day is coming.
¹⁴The wicked have drawn the sword and bent their bow to cast down the afflicted and the needy, to slay those who are upright in conduct.
¹⁵Their sword will enter their own heart, and their bows will be broken.
¹⁶Better is the little of the righteous than the abundance of many wicked.
¹⁷For the arms of the wicked will be broken, but the LORD sustains the righteous.
¹⁸The LORD knows the days of the blameless, and their inheritance will be forever.

THE BLESSED WOMAN

[19] They will not be ashamed in the time of evil, and in the days of famine they will have abundance.

[20] But the wicked will perish; and the enemies of the LORD will be like the glory of the pastures. They vanish—like smoke they vanish away.

[21] The wicked borrows and does not pay back, but the righteous is gracious and gives.

[22] For those blessed by Him will inherit the land, but hose cursed by Him will be cut off.

[23] The steps of a man are established by the LORD, and He delights in his way.

[24] When he falls, he will not be hurled headlong, because the LORD is the One who holds his hand.

[25] I have been young and now I am old, yet I have not seen the righteous forsaken or his descendants begging bread.

[26] All day long he is gracious and lends, and his descendants are a blessing.

[27] Depart from evil and do good, so you will abide forever.

[28] For the LORD loves justice and does not forsake His gold ones; They are preserved forever, but the descendants of the wicked will be cut off.

[29] The righteous will inherit the land and dwell in it forever.

[30] The mouth of the righteous utters wisdom, and his tongue speaks justice.

[31] The law of his God is in his heart; His steps do not slip.

[32] The wicked spies upon the righteous and seeks to kill him.

[34] The LORD will not leave him in his hand or let him be condemned when he is judged.

[35] Wait for the LORD and keep His way, and He will exalt you to inherit the land; When the wicked are cut off, you will see it.

[36] I have seen a wicked, violent man spreading himself like a luxuriant tree in its native soil,

[37] Then he passed away, and lo, he was no more; I sought for him, but he could not be found.

[38] Mark the blameless man, and behold the upright; For the man of peace will have posterity.

[39] But transgressors will be altogether destroyed; The posterity of the wicked will be cut off.

[40] But the salvation of the righteous is from the LORD; He is their strength in time of trouble.

[41] The LORD helps them and delivers them; He delivers them from the wicked and saves them, because they take refuge in Him.

Lesson Four
The Heart of Mercy

Day One

    I'll never forget those eyes! She sat there quietly blending into the sea of faces in the back of the crowded courtroom, the look of utter despair and hopelessness. Her face was shrouded with deep sorrow and the light in her eyes had been washed away by brokenness. She was a mother that had lost her only son in a senseless killing at the hands of a young teenage boy. Her son was a good and descent young man, a Christian who had set his heart to serve the Lord with his life. He was in the prime of his life when he was taken from this world. The trial went on for weeks and every day this mother would slip in and sit in the same place until the judge dismissed for the day. She would slip out as quietly as she came in, never saying a word to anyone. Neither before nor during the entire trial did she give an interview and she never spoke of her son's death. She was the picture of quiet strength and dignity as I had never seen before in the midst of great sorrow.
    Finally, the day came and the jury was sent out to decide the young man's fate. He was being tried as an adult and the prosecutors were seeking the death penalty. For days the jury deliberated the evidence and eventually came to an agreement. The foreman for the jury stood up before the judge and the

hundreds who had packed into the courtroom that morning and read these words: *"We, the jury, find the defendant...guilty of murder in the first degree."* There were mixed reactions that erupted in the courtroom but over all the noise there was one sound resounding above all others. It was the sound of wailing. It was not coming from the mother of the accused. It was coming from that grieving mother in the back of the courtroom who had lost her only son. This mother who had shown no emotion in public all this time was now overcome with tears and great sobbing. The judge called for a recess until the next morning when the young man would be sentenced. This mother gathered herself together and stood as graceful and heroic as anyone could, and asked the judge if could she speak. The judge was deeply moved and so he granted her request. The woman pulled from her pocket a piece of paper bearing these words and read them aloud: *"I know that you, honorable judge, have the power to take this boy's life and you have the power to save it. I beg you, honorable judge, to show him mercy by sparing his life. Who I am to ask you to withhold mercy when God did not withhold mercy from me?"*

I have thought about this woman many times over the years and every time my heart is moved and reminded of the greatness of mercy when it is given at such a great price. Jesus spoke of mercy that day to a crowd that included some who had experienced great sorrow. What does it mean to extend mercy and how can we give mercy when it is almost unbearable? Well, we are going to sit at the feet of Jesus, the merciful One, and see what He says. Pray before you begin, beloved, and ask God to teach you how to be merciful.

As always, let's begin by reading through Matthew Chapters 5, 6 and 7. I love to soak and soak and keep soaking in God's word. Once you're finished, I want you to locate Matthew 5:7 and write out this "blessed" in the space provided. This is the beatitude we will be looking at today and tomorrow. I've started it for you.

Matthew 5:7
"Blessed are the _____

_____."

If I were to ask you to write out in your own words what it means to be merciful, what would you say? How would you describe someone who is merciful?

_____

_____

Turn to your Word Windows Section in the back of your book and locate the definition for **"Merciful"** and write it out in the space provided for you.

Merciful

_____

_____

Based on the meaning of the word **"Merciful"**, would you say that it is an action or just an inward feeling? Why or why not?

_____

_____

I want us to look at a parable that Jesus shared with Peter one day. Parables are stories or illustrations that are told to teach us something; to reveal a spiritual truth. Jesus often spoke in parables to His disciples. Take a moment and read through Matthew 18:21-35 which is typed out for you at the end of this week's lesson. We will be studying this story in depth during our time together today. Once you've read through it go back through it again but this time, I want you to draw a circle around every reference to "mercy" or "compassion" with the color of your choice.

THE BLESSED WOMAN

How was mercy expressed in this story?

_____

_____

What was the reason for extending mercy given by the king to the slave in verses 27 and 32?

_____

_____

How much does it say that the first slave owed his lord in verse 24?

_____

How much were we told that the fellow slave owed in verse 28?

_____

The slave owed the king ten thousand talents. It's important to understand that ONE talent equaled 15 years worth of wages! So you do the math, beloved: 10,000 talents x 15 years. This was obviously a debt that the slave would have never been able to repay in his lifetime. It was an unforgivable debt in the eyes of man because it could never be repaid. The fellow slave only owed 100 denarii, which is equivalent to 3 months' wages. Do you see the difference in these two debts, beloved? One was forgiven a debt that he could never have repaid and yet he wasn't even willing to extend mercy to another who only owed him a very small debt that could have been paid in time.

Read verse 31 of this passage once more. I have typed it out for you so it will stand alone.

"So when his fellow slaves saw what had happened, they were deeply grieved and came and reported to their lord all that had happened."

According to this verse, when the wicked slave did not show mercy to his fellow slave, did it affect others and if so, how? How did they respond to what they saw?

_____

_____

This verse tells us that because the wicked slave did not show mercy as he was shown mercy, those who witnessed it were: **"deeply grieved."** These are convicting words, aren't they, beloved? The slave's lack of mercy brought grief to the hearts of others not so much because the slave did not show mercy, but because the slave received great mercy when he didn't deserve it and then refused to extend even a little mercy to someone else. This action deeply grieved the other slaves and it angered the king, but how does God feel when he sees this in us? Write out verse 35 of this passage in the space provided for you.

- **Matthew 18:35**

_____

_____

_____

What action does God take toward those who do as this slave did?

_____

In this parable Jesus tells us that He is describing the Kingdom of Heaven for us. We see this in verse 23. In the light of this comparison we can understand that the king or the lord in this story is God who is over the Kingdom of Heaven and that God is merciful no matter how great the debt a person may have. Look up the following verses and write down what you learned about God from each.

- **Hosea 6:6** (the word "loyalty" can be translated "mercy")

_____

_____

- **II Chronicles 30:9** (the word "compassionate" can be translated "merciful")

_____

_____

- **Ephesians 2:4**

_____

_____

- **Psalm 119:156**

_____

_____

- **Romans 9:15**

_____

_____

Let me ask you a question, beloved: Has anyone ever extended mercy to God? Has God ever received mercy? Why or why not?

_____

_____

_____

We could literally exhaust ourselves searching through the Word of God and never drain the fountain of God's endless mercy that is written in its pages for us. God is a merciful God because He chooses to be merciful. We saw this so clearly in Romans 9:15. Yes, it's true, God is merciful in nature but God has the right to choose not to be merciful. The reason He can chose to be merciful is because no one has ever extended mercy to Him! I don't want you to miss this truth, beloved! God isn't merciful because He is obligated to be. He is merciful because He chooses to be! In this parable we see this same truth. The king chose to be merciful. The slave did have a choice to be merciful because he had been extended mercy. When we are given mercy, beloved, we are commanded to give it in return. To beget mercy is to give mercy in the eyes of God. This is the foundational principle of mercy…

Principle
Those who have received mercy are obligated to extend mercy

I have typed out Matthew 18:33 for you to read through. Look at it closely, beloved, and let these powerful words that Jesus shared soak into your heart and soul. Read them aloud over and over again until they are part of your very being.

"Should you not also have had mercy on your fellow slave, in the same way that I had mercy on you?"

Those words are full of conviction: *"Should you not also have mercy"*… When someone receives mercy they are commanded by God to be merciful in return. We lost our right to withhold mercy at the cross of Calvary, beloved, because it was there we received mercy in full. You and I are under obligation to give mercy because we have been given mercy from God. What a reflection of mercy we see in the heart of God to know that He did not have to give mercy, but He desired to give it, and give it freely. Mercy given freely is the most sacrificial act of love there is. Knowing that we have received mercy and that we are obligated to extend mercy, then the following is true…

Benefit
Our right to withhold mercy is lost

Romans 9:23 says…

"And He did so to make known the riches of His glory upon vessels of mercy, which He prepared beforehand for glory."

We are vessels of God's mercy. Mercy is not a choice for us, beloved, because we have been given mercy. The moment we became a vessel of God's mercy we lost our right to withhold mercy from others. I pray you will let this truth permeate your being until you have laid hold of it in your heart. Many Christians live their entire life never grasping this truth. When a vessel of sin receives mercy then that vessel is transformed into a vessel of glory! Where sin was once seen, the glory of God floods into its place because sin cannot remain where mercy is present. The mercy of God knows no boundaries, precious student, and only mercy can transform an ordinary vessel into a vessel that illuminates the glory and beauty of a merciful, loving God.

One more thing, beloved, before we stop for today. Below is our memory verse for this week. Read over it at least three times so you can begin to commit it to memory.

Memory Verse

Romans 9:17

"… For this very purpose I raised you up, to demonstrate My power in you, and that My name might be proclaimed throughout the whole earth."

You have been diligent today, precious student. Oh, the wonderful truths that God has shown to us today through His Word. Rest now and meditate on all that God has shown you and I will see you on Day Two!

Day Two

Welcome back, beloved student. As you recall, yesterday we began looking at mercy and what it means to be merciful. Today, we want to continue to study mercy, but before we begin, let's take a moment and review what we learned. We saw through the parable of Jesus that when a person is given mercy they are commanded by God to give mercy in return. The person who receives mercy becomes a vessel of mercy and loses all rights to withhold mercy from another. We saw the very heart of God that desires to extend mercy even though He is not obligated to. Is all of this sounding familiar, beloved? Before we continue, take a moment to pray, asking God to open the eyes of your understanding that you may behold wonderful truths from His Word. We have a wonderful day ahead of us!

Do you remember what Jesus told the crowd that day about those who were merciful? Can you finish the verse below?

"Blessed are the _____, for they shall receive_____."

What is the promise given to those who are merciful?

_____

Mercy is a constant flow, beloved. We receive it, we give it, and it returns back to us to give out again. Mercy is to be a fountain that is continually flowing. The streams of mercy are never to run dry for they will never lack supply. As you remember, we studied the parable of the king and the slaves on Day One. Turn to the end of this lesson and locate Matthew 18:21-35 where this parable is given and take a moment to read through it. Once you've finished, I want you to write out verse 33 in the space provided.

- **Matthew 18:33**

_____

_____

_____

According to this verse, how was this slave to show mercy?

_____

If you answered, **"In the same way as he had been shown mercy,"** then you are right, beloved. The king told the wicked slave that he should have shown mercy to his fellow slave in the same way that the King had shown him mercy. This is God's command to us: Not only to show mercy because we have been given mercy, but to… *"Show mercy in the same way that I have shown mercy to you."*

If we are to know how we are to show mercy, then we must understand how we have been shown mercy. On Day One we learned the foundational principle of mercy. Today we are going to learn the standard of mercy; the standard that God lays out for us to follow.

How have we been shown mercy, beloved? Let's look at some passages that will give us some insight. As you look up each one, note what you learn about God's mercy. Note what God has done for us and how He has shown mercy. Also, it's important to note that mercy can be translated as compassion or loving kindness in scripture, depending on the version you use. Don't let the use of these words confuse you because they all have the same meaning.

- **Psalm 103:1-12**

_____

_____

_____

- **Titus 3:5**

- **Romans 5:6-8**

- **Psalm 136:1**

- **I John 1:9**

- **II Corinthians 5:14-15 & 21**

_____

_____

_____

Do you see the heart of God beloved? God is rich in mercy and mercy is ever reaching and extending itself fully to all those God sets His affections upon. God's mercy can never be measured, it can't be explained and it can never be repaid. We will never be worthy of God's mercy because God doesn't owe us anything. Oh the heart of God toward you and me precious student. Mercy is always active; it is never passive. This is the why the beauty of mercy is rarely seen because…

Principle
Mercy reveals the heart of God

Every time mercy is expressed; every time it is extended, it is revealing the very heart of God to the one who is receiving the mercy. Mercy is the heart of God. At the end of this week's study you will find Nehemiah 9:9-21 typed out for you. I want you to take a moment and read through this passage noting God's heart toward His people. Just to help you understand what is happening, it's important for you to know that these verses are like a walk down memory lane. Through a cupbearer named Nehemiah, God reminds the people of Israel all that He has done and all they have done. In this reminder, the heart of God is seen so beautifully and we get a view of mercy from God's perspective. Take your time reading through these verses. Read through it twice if you need to and I will meet you back here.

Isn't this a beautiful picture of the heart of God? God's heart is always to do good toward His people and not harm. Every time I read this passage I am reminded of my own life, and how God has always dealt kindly with me, exercising great forbearance and love. I stand in awe of the depth of God's mercy and grace. I believe that if you look close enough you will see your own life in these verses, for I believe we can all relate to this story in one way or another. To get a deeper look at the heart of God, I want you to take a purple colored pencil and draw a triangle around every reference to God. These will always be capitalized so they should be easy to spot. Remember, in doing this you are getting to know your Heavenly Father in a deeper way than before. We can never exhaust the knowledge of who God is. Getting to know God will be a lifetime journey that we'll take together until He calls you home. This knowledge can never be taken away from you once your heart has learned it because He taught it to you. God is a very personal teacher.

Once you've finished marking every reference to God, I want you to make a list of all the things that God had done for His people. This will take some time but it will be well worth the effort. When you begin to write out the things that God did for His people you will be amazed at the goodness of God. There is space provided below for you to list the truths you find.

God Has Done

_____

_____

_____

_____

_____

Every time you extend mercy, you are showing these same characteristics that we have just seen. True mercy will always express the true nature of God. Have others seen God expressed through your life? You cannot be extending true mercy and not be revealing the heart of God in the process. Mercy will never hide who God is, but rather it will uncover who He is. Every time we see mercy we are seeing the very heart of God. Mercy gives us a glimpse into The Holy One and it beckons us to follow.

Because mercy is an expression of the heart of God, then…

Benefit
The heart of God is seen every time we extend mercy

This may sound so simple, beloved, but it is a very profound truth. Stop with me a moment and meditate upon these words: **"Man can know the heart of God."** This is profound because God is a holy God who reigns in heaven. How can we, His creation made of dust, know His heart? How can we dare come so close as to peer into the chambers of the heart of Jehovah? It's called mercy, beloved! God so wants us to know His heart that He extends mercy to even the most sinful of people so we, thousands of years later, can come along and read about it and in the reading see the very heart of God laid bare before us. God extends mercy not only to reveal mercy, but also to reveal the richness of His glory. Do you remember our verse from Romans 9:23? Let's look at it once more together because I feel it fits so appropriately here with what we have just learned. I've typed it out for you to read.

Romans 9:23 *says...*

"And He did so to make known the riches of His glory upon vessels of mercy, which He prepared beforehand for glory."

What a God we have, beloved! What a God we have. His mercies are new every morning. He has loved us with an everlasting love that can never be exhausted. As we come to a close in our study time together, I want you to take a moment and just spend some time thanking God for the mercy He has shown you. You may also want to review your memory verse.

I love you so much, precious student. I will look for you on Day Three.

Day Three

Take a few minutes to pray before you begin your study time today, beloved. As you remember from yesterday, mercy is an expression of the very heart of God and every time mercy is given, the heart of God is seen. Mercy in action is a way for mankind to understand who God is and what He is like.

In order for us to be able to understand this truth, we began looking at Nehemiah 9:9-21 on Day Two. Today, we want to continue studying this passage so we can come to know the heart of God in an even deeper way. Let's begin our study time together by reading through this passage again to refresh our memories. Remember, you have already marked every reference to God. Turn to the end of this week's study and locate this passage of scripture so you can review it.

Once you finished reading through these verses, write out a description of God based on Nehemiah 9:9-21. It will help you to revisit the places where you marked your references for God. What characteristics of God did you see? What did you learn about God? How would you describe Him based on this passage?

What God Is Like

_____

_____

_____

_____

_____

From what we've seen so far, would you say that God's people had been shown mercy?

_____

Let's read through this passage once more, but this time mark every reference to the people by drawing a circle around each with the color of your choice. Once you've finished, make a list of what you learned about the people of God in this passage. What had been given to them and how had they responded to what was given to or done for them? Take your time on this, beloved, and make sure you don't miss anything.

God's People

_____

_____

_____

_____

_____

Did you see yourself, beloved? If you did, I understand. I see myself so clearly in the lives of these people. I, too, have been granted the rich mercy of God. I have experienced His goodness in my life and have turned away from Him, putting other things before and above Him. I have refused to listen at times and have forgotten His wondrous deeds. I have been stubborn and sought my own way more times than I can remember, yet God has continued to be merciful and kind to me, a sinner. Why would God do this, beloved? Have you ever stopped to think about this? I have often thought, as I have read through this passage, *"God, why did you put up with them?"* And even more so, *"God, why have you put up with me?"*

Let me take you to a passage of scripture that God gave me as His answer. Turn to Ezra 9:5-9 and read through it a couple of times. In this passage Ezra has just been made aware of the sin of God's people and as you will see, he is deeply grieved because of it.

According to these verses, what had been given to God's people for a brief moment of time?

_____

Turn to your Word Windows Section and look up the word for **"Grace"** as used here and write out its definition in the space provided.

Grace

Isn't this what we see God doing here in Ezra and what we saw Him doing in Nehemiah? God bent down to bestow kindness to those who were inferior, in other words to those who were undeserving of it. This is what mercy does, beloved. Mercy finds its heart in the chambers of grace. Grace, in its simplest form, means unmerited favor. God lovingly reminds me that this is who He is and His ways are not my ways, praise God! Aren't you glad that God is not like us, beloved? None of us would be shown mercy if it were up to us, would we? But it's not up to us, is it? This is the second foundational principle of mercy...

Principle
Mercy is not based on the worthiness of the recipient but on the worthiness of God

Mercy is based on Who God is, not on who man is. We often withhold mercy because we feel the person doesn't deserve it. We base our actions on the merits of others and not on the merits of God and what He is worthy of. This way of thinking will never accomplish the work of God and can never bring the glory to God that He so justly deserves. This is why mercy can never be withheld... because God will always be worthy. None of us will ever be worthy of anyone's mercy let alone the mercy of God. The question is: **"Do you believe God is worthy?"** This is a question, beloved, that finds its answer in how you live your life. So what answer would we find if we surveyed the way you live and how you act toward others? It gives you something to think on, doesn't it?

Do you remember the day God saved you...the day He forgave you of all of your sins? Has God ever been a light for you in the midst of darkness, showing you the way when you had no idea where to go? Has He ever provided for you financially or physically? Has He ever forsaken you, beloved, even when you may have forsaken Him? Has God ever failed you? Have there been times when you have forgotten the goodness of God toward you? Has God ever rescued you from the enemy?

Over and over throughout scripture, we see that God calls His people to remember what He has done and they are warned not to forget the mighty deeds of God. Every time God's people failed to remember the goodness of God, they turned away from following Him. So, beloved, take time now to remember the wondrous deeds of a mighty, merciful God who has followed you all the days of your life. Why don't you take God by the hand and ask Him to walk your mind and heart through the memories you have made together. It will be the sweetest walk you've ever taken, beloved, and one that will renew your faith and love for God in a powerful way.

As you take this memory walk with God, why don't you write down how God has shown you mercy through out your life? I understand this will take time and thought.

Memory Lane of Mercy

_____

_____

_____

_____

_____

You see, precious student, when we survey our lives we find that goodness and mercy have followed us every day. How will we ever see that if we never take time to pause and reflect back on what God has done? It was never based on who we were or are or will even become some day, but it was based on who God is and that He is worthy. The truth is that none of us would ever receive mercy because we are not worthy. Romans 3:10-12 tells us:

"There is none righteous, not even one; there is none who understands, there is none who seeks for God; all have turned aside, together they have become useless; there is none who does good, there is not even one."

Aren't you thankful that the determining factor for receiving mercy will always be because of who God is and not what we are? This is the power of mercy.

Because mercy is based on the worthiness of God and not man then...

Benefit
Mercy has no bounds

The supply of mercy will never be exhausted because God will forever be worthy. When we embrace the truth and let this benefit take place then we are pleasing and honorable to God. Mercy should always look through the eyes of God and not the eyes of man.

Take a moment and turn to the Blessed Chart found in the back of your book and write down this new "blessed" that we've learned. If you have a little time you might want to read over your memory verse.

See you on Day Four beloved. Thank you for studying God's Word with me today.

Day Four

Welcome back, beloved, to our last day of study this week. As we have journeyed through this week's lesson together I have prayed that you have been refreshed and challenged by the truths God has shown us regarding mercy. There have been times in my life when I have refused to extend mercy because I felt that the person was not worthy to receive mercy. As we have seen this week, mercy is not ours to withhold because it comes from God. Today, as we conclude our study on mercy, I want us to look at the reason behind mercy. Why did God choose to show us mercy when He did not have to? What was God's purpose behind extending mercy? What should be the driving force for us to extend mercy? To find the answers, we must go to the place where mercy is found. It's to the most sacred place mentioned in the Bible. So today, precious student, we are on a journey. Today's journey can change your life if you listen from the depths of your heart.

Let's stop and take time to pray, precious student, asking God to unveil the eyes of our understanding. I am bowing my knee with you right now as I am writing this so when you stop and pray you can know that someone has gone before you to the throne of God on your behalf.

We'll begin our study by journeying back to the life of Moses when he led the people of Israel. Turn to the back of this week's study and locate the passage of scripture for Exodus 25:1-22 that is typed out for you there. This will be our main focus of scripture for study today. Take time to read through these verses to familiarize yourself with the text. In this passage the people of Israel have just been delivered out of the land of Egypt by God. God has led them to Mount Sinai and He has called for Moses to come up on the mountain to meet with Him. Moses was up on this mountain for forty days and forty nights and during this time God gave to him the Ten Commandments. He also gave him instructions about many things, including how to erect the tabernacle where they were to worship God and make atonements for their sins. Chapter 25 is the beginning of these instructions. Take time now to read through these verses.

Let's read through this passage once more. This time take a color pencil of your choice and draw a rectangle around every reference to the mercy seat.

What did you learn about the mercy seat by marking the text?

_____

_____

_____

According to verse 22, what two things will happen at the mercy seat? What will God do there in this place?

1. _____

2. _____

The mercy seat was a pretty special place, beloved, for it was where God was going to meet and speak with man. Turn in your Bible to Hebrews Chapter

Nine and read verses 1-7. We are not going to study the tabernacle in detail in this study, but rather we want to focus primarily on the mercy seat. According to these verses, where was the mercy seat, which is part of the Ark of the Covenant, located?

_____

Who was the only one that was allowed to come into the Holy of Holies and how often?

_____

Hebrews is the only place where the word **"Mercy"** is used in the New Testament. Turn to your Word Windows Section and find the definition of mercy seat and record it in the space provided for you.

Mercy Seat

_____

_____

In the meaning of **"Mercy"** we saw the word *"propitiation"*. This word gives us a beautiful picture of what happens at the mercy seat. The Greek word for propitiation is the same Greek word for mercy seat, so you can use these two words interchangeably since they mean the same thing.

Webster's definition of *"propitiation"* is: "to cause to become favorably inclined. To win or regain the good will of. It means to appease or satisfy."

The following verses will help give us further insight into the meaning of the word "propitiation." Look up these verses in your Bible and record what you learn about propitiation from each.

- **Romans 3:23-25**

_____

_____

_____

- **I John 2:1-2**

_____

_____

_____

- **I John 4:9-10**

_____

_____

_____

Based on these verses and our word studies what do you think the mercy seat was for? In other words, how would you describe the mercy seat to someone who doesn't know what it is? Take your time, beloved, and think through everything we've seen so far.

_____

_____

_____

Based on everything we've seen so far, why do you think it was called the mercy seat?

_____

_____

Take a moment and read Exodus 25:8 which is typed out for you below.

Exodus 25:8

"Let them make Me a sanctuary, that I may dwell among them."

According to Exodus 25:8, why did God want them to construct a sanctuary?

_____

What does this show us about the heart of God? Where does He desire to be?

_____

_____

I love the amplified version of Exodus 25:22 that refers to the mercy seat and I want to share it with you. I think it will be a blessing to you as it has been to me.

Exodus 25:22 (Amplified Bible)

"There I will meet with you and, from above the Mercy Seat, from between the two cherubim that are upon the Ark of the Testimony (or covenant), I will speak intimately with you of all which I will give you in commandment to the Israelites."

You see, beloved, the mercy seat was in the Holy of Holies. Only the High Priest could enter there after he had made atonement for his own sins. The Holy of Holies was just that, the most holy place, for this is where God would come down. The Holy of Holies was the dwelling place of God. On the mercy seat the High Priest would place the sacrifice that was being offered up for the atonement of sins and God would come down and consume the sacrifice if it was pleasing in His sight. The mercy seat was the place where Holiness would come together with sinful man. It brought man into the presence of God because God wanted to be close to us.

If I were to ask you why God extended mercy when He was not obligated to, what would you say, beloved? Think of what we've learned concerning God. What was His reason behind giving mercy when He was not obligated to?

God said that He would meet with man at the mercy seat. Turn to your Word Windows Section and find the definition for **"meet"** and write it out in the space provided for you.

Meet

Did you get it, beloved? When God said He was going to "meet" with man there at the seat of mercy, He was saying that He was going to betroth Himself to man. Mercy is God setting His affection upon you; giving His very heart to you. How awesome is that thought, oh daughter, that a Holy God would want to join Himself to us! Just as a man and woman come together as one in Holy Matrimony, so God came together with us at the mercy seat. So what does mercy do?

Principle
Mercy removes the separation between God and man

Isn't mercy a beautiful picture of the heart of God? How deep, how wide, how high and how rich is the mercy of God. We will never be fully able to grasp this until we get to heaven, but we can know right at this moment that the heart of God loves you and me, and His heart's greatest desire is to be with us. Mercy is the bridge that allows man to come to God. Mercy is the union between us and God and the wonder of it all is that God initiated it.

To see this life changing benefit of mercy, turn in your Bible to Hebrews 10:19-22 and take a moment to read through these verses. According to verse 22 of this passage, what can we do?

So, beloved daughter, because mercy removes the separation between man and God then…

Benefit
We can draw near to God

Oh, how God loves you and I! How He longs to be with us and to love us with an unconditional love. We will learn more about this in our lesson time together, beloved. Let's take a few moments and review the principles and benefits that we have learned from God's Word this week.

Week in Review

Principle # 1: *Those who have received mercy are obligated to extend mercy*
Benefit: *Our right to withhold mercy is gone*

Principle # 2: *Mercy reveals the heart of God*
Benefit: *The heart of God is seen every time mercy is extended*

Principle #3: *Mercy is not based on the worthiness of the recipient, but on the worthiness of God*
Benefit: *Mercy has no bounds*

Principle #4: *Mercy removes the separation between God and man*
Benefit: *We can draw near to God*

As we wrap up our week, let me leave you with a few questions.

Personal Evaluation

Are there people in your life that you have withheld mercy from?

Do you believe you have the right to withhold mercy, beloved?

Have you looked at mercy through the eyes of God?

Have you forgotten the mercy that God has shown you throughout your life?

These are all questions we should continually ask ourselves. To withhold mercy from others is a sin against a merciful God. A fitting closure to this week's lesson would be to finish our time together on our knees thanking God for who He is and for the heart He has toward us. Will you bow your knee with me right now, daughter? Thank you so much for the time you are giving to learn about your God. How I pray you will embrace the truths you are learning. In doing so, your life will never be the same.

Much love to you my precious friend.

Matthew 18:21-35

[21] Then Peter came and said to Him, "Lord, how often shall my brother sin against me and I forgive him? Up to seven times? "

[22] Jesus said to him, "I do not say to you, up to seven times, but up to seventy times seven.

[23] "For this reason the kingdom of heaven may be compared to a king who wished to settle accounts with his slaves.

[24] "When he had begun to settle them, one who owed him ten thousand talents was brought to him.

[25] "But since he did not have the means to repay, his lord commanded him to be sold, along with his wife and children and all that he had, and repayment to be made.

[26] "So the slave fell to the ground and prostrated himself before him, saying, 'Have patience with me and I will repay you everything.'

[27] "And the lord of that slave felt compassion and released him and forgave him the debt.

[28] "But that slave went out and found one of his fellow slaves who owed him a hundred denarii; and he seized him and began to choke him, saying, 'Pay back what you owe.'

[29] "So his fellow slave fell to the ground and began to plead with him, saying, 'Have patience with me and I will repay you.'

[30] "But he was unwilling and went and threw him in prison until he should pay back what was owed.

[31] "So when his fellow slaves saw what had happened, they were deeply grieved and came and reported to their lord all that had happened.

[32] "Then summoning him, his lord said to him, 'You wicked slave, I forgave you all that debt because you pleaded with me.

[33] 'Should you not also have had mercy on your fellow slave, in the same way that I had mercy on you?'

[34] "And his lord, moved with anger, handed him over to the torturers until he should repay all that was owed him.

[35] "My heavenly Father will also do the same to you, if each of you does not forgive his brother from your heart."

THE BLESSED WOMAN

Nehemiah 9:9-21

[9]"You saw the affliction of our fathers in Egypt, and heard their cry by the Red Sea.

[10]"Then You performed signs and wonders against Pharaoh, against all his servants and all the people of his land; for You knew that they acted arrogantly toward them, and made a name for Yourself as it is this day.

[11]"You divided the sea before them, so they passed through the midst of the sea on dry ground; and their pursuers You hurled into the depths, like a stone into raging waters.

[12]"And with a pillar of cloud You led them by day, and with a pillar of fire by night to light for them the way in which they were to go.

[13]"Then You came down on Mount Sinai, and spoke with them from heaven; You gave them just ordinances and true laws, good statutes and commandments.

[14]"So You made known to them Your holy Sabbath, and laid down for them commandments, statutes and law, through Your servant Moses.

[15]"You provided bread from heaven for them for their hunger, You brought forth water from a rock for them for their thirst, and You told them to enter in order to possess the land which You swore to give them.

[16]"But they, our fathers, acted arrogantly; they became stubborn and would not listen to Your commandments.

[17]"They refused to listen, and did not remember Your wondrous deeds which You had performed among them; so they became stubborn and appointed a leader to return to their slavery in Egypt. But you are a God of forgiveness, gracious and compassionate, slow to anger and abounding in loving-kindness; and You did not forsake them.

[18]"Even when they made for themselves a calf of molten metal and said, This is your God who brought you up from Egypt,'

[19]"You, in Your great compassion, did not forsake them in the wilderness; the pillar of cloud did not leave them by day, to guide them on their way, Nor the pillar of fire by night, to light for them the way in which they were to go.

[20]"You gave Your good Spirit to instruct them, your manna you did not withhold from their mouth, and You gave them water for their thirst.

[21]"Indeed, forty years You provided for them in the wilderness and they were not in want; their clothes did not wear out, nor did their feet swell.

Exodus 25:1-22

¹Then the Lord spoke to Moses, saying,

²"Tell the sons of Israel to raise a contribution for Me; from every man whose heart moves him you shall raise My contribution.

³"This is the contribution which you are to raise from them: gold, silver and bronze.

⁴"Blue, purple and scarlet material, fine linen, goat hair,

⁵"Rams' skins dyed red, porpoise skins, acacia wood,

⁶"Oil for lighting, spices for the anointing oil and for the fragrant incense,

⁷"Onyx stones and setting stones for the ephod and for the breastpiece.

⁸"Let them construct a sanctuary for Me, that I may dwell among them.

⁹"According to all that I am going to show you, as the pattern for the tabernacle and the pattern of all its furniture, just so you shall construct it.

¹⁰"They shall construct and ark of acacia wood two and a half cubits long, and one and a half cubits wide, and one and a half cubits high.

¹¹"You shall overlay it with pure gold, inside and out you shall overlay it, and you shall make a gold molding around it.

¹²"You shall cast four gold rings for it and fasten them on its four feet, and two rings shall be one side of it and two rings on the other side of it.

¹³"You shall make poles of acacia wood and overlay them with gold.

¹⁴"You shall put the poles into the rings on the sides of the ark, to carry the ark with them.

¹⁵"The poles shall remain in the rings of the ark; they shall not be removed from it.

¹⁶"You shall put into the ark the testimony which I shall give you.

¹⁷"You shall make a mercy seat of pure gold, two and a half cubits long and one and a half cubits wide.

¹⁸"You shall make two cherubim of gold, make them of hammered work at the two ends of the mercy seat.

¹⁹"Make one cherub at one end and one cherub at the other end; you shall make the cherubim of one piece with the mercy seat at its two ends.

²⁰"The cherubim shall have their wings spread upward, covering the mercy seat with their wings and facing one another; the faces of the cherubim are to be turned toward the mercy seat.

[21]"You shall put the mercy seat on top of the ark, and in the ark you shall put the testimony which I will give to you.

[22]"There I will meet with you; and from above the mercy seat, from between the two cherubim which are upon the ark of the testimony, I will speak to you about all that I will give you in commandment for the sons of Israel.

LESSON FIVE
A Heart that Is Pure

Day One

If I were to pull back your outer shell, beloved; if I could open up your heart leaving it completely exposed, what would I see there? I don't think any one of us would want someone to see what was in our hearts, would we? But there is one who does see all and nothing is hidden from Him. I Samuel 16:7 tells us: *"God sees not as man sees, for man looks at the outward appearance, but the Lord looks at the heart."* God doesn't care what we look like on the outside, but He cares very deeply about what is on the inside. He searches and tries the heart of man to see what is there. Only God can do that, beloved. He will always look straight to your heart in all things. He knows what's on the inside of your heart will always determine what's on the outside. There are no secrets hidden from Him.

Jesus spoke about the heart of man that day up on the hillside and the words He spoke were some of the most powerful words ever spoken. Today, we are going to bend near and listen to what Jesus said to His listeners regarding the heart of man. Take a moment to pray before you begin your study.

Turn in your Bible to Matthew 5:8 and write it out in the space provided for you. I've started it for you.

THE BLESSED WOMAN

Matthew 5:8

"Blessed are the _____

_____ *"*

From this verse, what kind of heart will the blessed person have?

_____

Turn to your Word Windows Section located in the back of your study book and find the definition for **"pure"**. Once you've located it, write it out in the space provided for you.

Pure

_____

_____

Based on the meaning of **"pure"** what do you think Jesus meant when He said: *"Blessed are the pure in heart?"* What kind of heart would this person have? What would their characteristics or their lifestyle be like?

_____

_____

_____

Look up the following verses and note what you learn from each one about purity and those who are pure.

- Proverbs 21:8

- Proverbs 30:12

- II Timothy 2:22

- I Peter 1:22

- Philippians 4:8

We can understand from scripture that having a pure heart is having a heart that is without blemish; a heart that has no sin…a heart that is spotless and clean before God. If a pure heart were opened up and laid bare before God, He would find nothing in it that would condemn. This leaves us with one question. How can we have a heart that is pure in the eyes of God? Is it possible, beloved? To help us find these answers, I want us to look at Psalm 51:1-17 which is typed out for you at the end of this week's lesson.

Before we do that, let me give you the setting for this Psalm. King David had sinned by having an affair with a married woman and then this woman became pregnant. He then, in an attempt to hide his sin, had the woman's husband killed in a battle. But as David found out, you cannot cover up sin because it will find you out. For a while David thought he had gotten away with his sin, but some time later a prophet named Nathan, who had been sent by God, came and confronted David about what he had done.

David ended up paying a great price for his sins; a price David never intended to pay. This Psalm, this prayer, was a result of David coming clean with everything he had done. Read through this passage, taking your time to see the heart of a king who had sinned so greatly. Once you are finished, we will look at it more closely together.

Take a colored pencil of your choice and draw a box around each reference to King David in this passage.

What did you learn about David by marking the text? Revisit every place you marked and list the things you saw in the space provided for you.

King David

_____

_____

_____

_____

What do you think King David's greatest desire was as seen in this passage? What do we learn about the heart of David in these verses?

_____

_____

_____

According to verse 7, what was David asking God to do?

_____

David not only acknowledged his sin before God but He recognized his need to be purified. David knew that he needed a pure heart. Read verse 10 of this passage and write out what David was asking the Lord to do within him.

_____

David could have stopped at the confessing of his sin and crying out for forgiveness, but he doesn't do that. David takes his cry a step farther by asking the Lord to, *"Create in me a clean heart."* These are powerful words when studied closely. What was David asking God to do? To help us understand, let's look up the meaning of the word **"create"** in the Word Windows Section. Once you've located it, write out the meaning in the space provided.

Create

_____

_____

Based on the meaning of the word **"create"**, what do you think David was asking God to do when he asked Him to create within him a clean heart? What was David acknowledging by asking God to do this? Take your time, beloved, to think about your answer.

_____

_____

_____

You see, beloved, David wasn't asking the Lord to restore his heart; he was asking the Lord to make in him a brand new heart. A heart that was clean. To make something out of nothing! Only God could do that. David knew that his heart was so sinful and so marred, so stained with the guilt and shame of his sin, that he needed for Creator God to start all over within him and create something new. You see, precious student, a brand new heart would have no past sins, no spots or blemishes; it would be pure. Remember our meaning for "pure?" It means without spot or blemish. It means to be clean. This was David's cry. He wanted a pure heart, a heart with no defects. The only way he could get this pure heart was to have God create one within him.

Beloved, this is the beginning of purity. It's recognizing, just as David did, that the heart of man is not pure as it is; it is not, nor will it ever be, without blemish, without sin. David cried out that he was born with a sinful heart. This was the beginning of the purifying process for King David for he saw himself as God saw him. This is the first fundamental principle of purity...

Principle
A pure heart must be created by God

Do you see this, beloved? David recognized that his heart was sinful on its own and he also recognized the need to have a pure heart. David went to the only One that could give him a pure heart and that was the Creator. The One who fashioned the heart of man, the One who is pure and holy. You see, precious student, sinful man cannot make within himself a holy and pure heart.

Only the hands of one who is pure can make a pure heart. God is that One. The moment that David cried out, "Create within me..." he was confessing his need for a new heart because the word he used means to make something out of nothing. David knew that there was nothing clean within him. He knew that he could not do this on his own. This is where the work of God begins within us: with our confession of total inability to help or change ourselves.

David knew a powerful secret when he used the word "create." He knew that whatever his heart needed he could ask God to create it within him. In David's case he needed to be made clean; he needed to be made pure. In other words, David needed a clean heart created within him because his sin had made it unclean. Do you see the power in this truth? What is it that you need right now, beloved? Is it a heart of love for your husband? Is it a heart of forgiveness toward someone else? Is it a heart of courage to face an insurmountable circumstance? Is it a heart of compassion? Is it a heart of peace because of the storm that is raging in your life? Maybe you are like David and you need a heart that is clean. Oh, beloved, God is able for He is the Creator God! David's sin was great, but it was not too great for God!

When we understand that God must create a new heart within us, then something powerful happens in our life...

Benefit
A new beginning can be found

David found this new beginning. He paid a price for his sin, but God granted him a new beginning by giving David a new heart. A new heart is a new beginning! It's the chance to start all over again. How amazing and beautiful is our God to do such a thing on our behalf. Let's personalize this truth, beloved. Take a moment and read the prayer below and fill in what it is that your heart might need at this point in your life.

"Dear God, create within me a heart of  **"**

As you know beloved, every week we are committing a verse to memory so that we will have the treasure of God's Word stored in our hearts and minds. This week's memory verse is Psalm 51:10. This is a verse that you will draw upon over and over in your walk with the Lord. Remember, precious student, whenever you recall this prayer of David, you can ask God for whatever your heart may need at the moment, just as we did just a minute ago. Take a few minutes and read over our verse for this week. See you on Day Two!

Memory Verse

Psalm 51:10

"Create within me a clean heart, O God, and renew a steadfast spirit within me."

Day Two

"Blessed are the pure in heart, for they shall see God.". What powerful words these are. Do you realize what Jesus was saying to the crowd of people that day? He was telling them how they could see God, how they could see Jehovah. I can't imagine the stir this must have caused in the minds and hearts of those who were there that day. If you were told how you could see God, would you do it? Would you believe it? I wonder how many grasped what Jesus was saying. This is our study theme today, beloved. Take time to kneel before the throne of God and ask Him to help you grasp this powerful truth that Jesus was speaking of. When we find this truth, precious student, we will see God.

I want us to begin our time together today by turning to Psalm 51:1-17 that is typed out for you at the end of this week's lesson. As you recall, we began studying these verses on Day One and we saw that David asked the Lord to create within him a clean heart. Today, I want us to look at what else David asked the Lord to do in this passage. Read through this passage once to re-familiarize yourself with the text. Once you are finished, I want you to read through it once more but this time I want you to underline every request that David made to God. Choose any color that makes the text stand out to you.

Now that you are through, make a list of everything that David asked God to do in his life.

David Requested of God

_____

_____

_____

_____

_____

According to verse 7 of this passage, what was David asking God to do?

_____

David was asking God to purify him and to wash him. I believe there are times in our lives when God purges us. This is what David was asking God to do; to purge him. Purging is not just a process. It is a painful process that requires a heart that truly yearns to be what God wants them to be. David desired above all to have a heart like God. From this desire flowed this courageous request to purge him. Purging is a removing of those things that should not be there; it is a refining process. It is much like the silversmith who refines silver.

Typed out for you below is Zechariah 13:9. In this passage, God is speaking to the nation of Israel about a future day…

Zechariah 13:9

"And I will bring the third part through the fire, refine them as silver is refined, and test them as gold is tested. They will call on My name and I will answer them; I will say, 'They are My people,' and they will say, 'The Lord is my God.'"

According these verses, what is God going to do to His people?

_____

_____

God is the great silver smith; the relentless refiner. I want us to look at one more passage which is found in Malachi 3:2-3.

Malachi 3:2-3

² *"But who can endure the day of His coming? And who can stand when He appears? For He is like a refiner's fire and like fullers' soap.*
³ *"He will sit as a smelter and purifier of silver and He will purify the sons of Levi and refine them like gold and silver, so that they may present to the Lord offerings in righteousness."*

What do these verses tell us about the Lord? What is He compared to?

_____

_____

Turn to your Word Windows Section and locate the definition for **"refine"** as used in these two passages. Once you've found it, record the meaning in the space provided for you.

Refine

_____

_____

Silver is a most precious metal that is magnificent in appearance when the light hits it at just the right angle causing a radiance of beauty and splendor. Only

God could make something so spectacular. What makes the silver so beautiful and so precious is not the finished product that we see when it is sold in the form of a ring, a necklace, a watch or a bracelet, but it is the process that took place to bring about the finished product. When silver is mined, it is in a natural state that does not reveal the beauty that is hidden beneath the surface. The silver smith will take the silver in this raw, natural state and begin a process that takes time and patience. He will place the silver in a melting pot and melt it down with fire.

When the silver is heated to a certain temperature something wonderful begins to happen. The impurities that are in the silver begin to rise to the top. These impurities are referred to as dross. As the dross rises to the top, the silver smith will scrape it off removing it from the silver. This is a very delicate process, because if the temperature is too hot or if he leaves the silver over the flame too long, then it will be ruined. The silver smith must take care that he does not leave the precious silver while he has it over the fire. He will continue this process until all the dross is gone. Look up the following verses and write out below what you learn from each.

- **Proverbs 25:4**

_____

_____

_____

- **Isaiah 1:25-26**

_____

_____

_____

- **Ezekiel 22:15-22**

___

___

___

- **Psalm 66:10**

___

___

___

- **Jeremiah 6:27-30**

___

___

___

Do you see, beloved, that God refines us in order to purify us. Our second principle of purity is…

Principle
A pure heart comes through refining

Look up Proverbs 27:19 and write it out in the space provided for you.

___

___

According to this verse, what does the heart of man reflect?

_____

Let me ask you a question, beloved. If the heart of man reflects man, then what would you think the heart of God would reflect?

_____

If you said, "God," then you are correct, beloved, for what is in a heart will reflect who that heart belongs to. The heart is a reflection of ownership. Can I ask you a question, precious student? Who owns your heart? Whose throne is set up there? Does God have your heart or have you given it to another?

Do you remember what the promise is for the pure in heart? Finish the verse below.

"Blessed are the pure in heart for _____."

Remember the blessed promise that Jesus made to the pure in heart? He said they will see God. How will the pure in heart see God? Of course we will see God when we get to heaven, but I also believe there is another promise of seeing God hidden in this beatitude. To help us see this, let me share something with you about the refining process. Let me start by asking you a question.

How does the silver smith know when the dross is gone? Each time the silver smith removes the dross that has risen to the top, he stops and looks into the silver to see if he can see his reflection. When the silver smith sees his reflection clearly in the silver he knows that all the dross is gone. You see, daughter, the beauty of the silver was there all along. It was just shrouded by the impurities, by the dross.

Who is our silver smith beloved?

_____

If you answered, "God," then you are right! We've seen that today in our study. So if God is our refiner, if He is the silver smith then how will God know when our heart is pure? It's the same way that the silver smith knows when the silver is ready. Do you remember?

Do you see it, beloved? God will know that our hearts are pure when He looks at us and sees Himself. So, how will the pure in heart see God? They will see it in themselves because they will be a reflection of God. What an awesome truth this is, precious student. What an incentive for us to become pure, as God would have us to. But God cannot be seen until the dross is brought out and then removed. Purity is a refining process that leads us to our benefit for today.

Because a pure heart comes through refining, then…

Benefit
The dross in your life will continue to be removed until God is seen

Refining is never easy. It is not something we would choose if left to ourselves because it is a painful process. Refining burns everything away, but only after it surfaces. Many times we want God to just remove things in our lives instantly. But the truth is that first God must surface things that are not holy. He must bring them to the surface. He must make them visible to us and then we must allow Him to remove them. Sometimes when God surfaces things, we look at them and we rebel by refusing to let God remove them. If we don't allow God to remove the dross once it is brought to the surface then the dross is what the people will see when they look at us. The dross will not go back down into the silver and hide itself as it did before. It will remain on the surface as a reminder of our need to have it removed. Just as removing the dross will reveal holiness, not removing the dross will reveal un-holiness. Dross it the reflection of what is in the heart of man; removing it is a reflection of what is in the heart of God.

As long as we are in this flesh body there will be areas in our lives, beloved, that we will fight to hang on to as the purging process takes place. This is the war that exists between the flesh and the Spirit of God that dwells in those who are His children. We see this truth in Galatians 5:17 which says: *"For the flesh sets its desire against the Spirit, and the Spirit against the flesh; for these are in opposition to one another, so that you may not do the things that you please."* This is when God intensifies the heat so He can take it from us. Purging is done with fire beloved and fire is all consuming. God tells us that He is a consuming fire (Deuteronomy 4:24... *"for the Lord thy God is a consuming fire!")* Every sacrifice that God accepted was through ashes.

With every beat of God's heart, He desires to have all of you. Upon the chambers of your heart, precious daughter, He inscribed the words... *This one belongs to Me.".* Why don't you take time to talk to God and ask Him to begin searching your heart so He can make it pure. Would you be so bold, beloved?

May God begin a refining process in you today and may His hand not be lifted until you are the very image of Him who created you. Remember, daughter, God created you in His image. We are to be like Him; a mirror of the Holy One.

Praising the Lord for you.

Day Three

As you know, we've been learning about purity of heart and what that means to us as God's children. We learned on Day Two of our study that the pure in heart will see God within themselves because they are being refined by the Holy Silver Smith. He will not stop until all is purged away from the heart of those who seek to be pure. We understand that having a pure heart is a process and one that God performs within us. God will use many different avenues to bring about this purging process in our lives. This is what we will look at today. What does God use to bring about purity? What does He do to surface the dross in our lives? We don't often recognize the things God uses to bring out the impurities in us that can cause us to miss the working of God in our lives.

How I have prayed for you, precious student that God will impart wisdom from His heart to yours. Are you ready to get started? Take time to pray, beloved, before you begin.

For the sake of review, let's begin our study by reading through Matthew Chapters 5-7. We haven't read through these chapters in a while and repetition is vital for retention, vital for sealing God's Word upon the tablets of our heart.

THE BLESSED WOMAN

Once you're finished reading, write out this week's "beatitude" or "blessed" that we have been learning about in the space provided.

"*Blessed are* _____

_____."

Take a moment and record this *"blessed"* on the Blessed Chart located in the back of your book.

Joel 2:12-13 is what is typed out for you. The only thing we know about Joel is that he was a prophet God used to call the nation of Israel to repentance for their sin. Their sin had taken their hearts far away from God and Joel was the voice God used to call them back.

Joel 2:12-13

¹²"Yet even now," declares the Lord, "Return to Me with all your heart, and with fasting, weeping and mourning;
¹³and rend your heart and not your garments."

According to these verses, what did God want His people to do? What was He saying about their hearts?

_____

_____

God tells His people to "rend" their heart and not their garments. Turn to your Word Windows Section located in the back of your book and find the definition for the word **"rend"**. Once you've located it, record the meaning in the space provided.

Rend

_____

_____

Based on our word study, what do you think God meant when He said, "…rend your heart and not your garment?"

_____

_____

Tearing ones clothes is an expression of grief…a symbol of remorse and it is seen through out the Word of God. God was telling His people that He wasn't interested in them tearing their clothes. Their garments, because they were grieving. God wanted their very hearts to be torn! Why? Because God wanted their hearts to belong completely to Him. He didn't want to be their God outwardly. He wanted to be their God inwardly. God wanted their hearts to be His throne.

For God to be our God inwardly He must purify our heart. It is a rending or a tearing out of all that is not of God. Look up the following verses and note the things that God uses in our lives to purify us…to rend our hearts.

- **Psalm 119:9-11**

_____

_____

_____

- **I Peter 5:8-10**

_____

_____

_____

- **James 1:2-4**

- **Daniel 11:35**

- **James 3:2-3**

One more, beloved student!

- **Ezekiel 18:30-31**

As you can see, God uses many things to cleanse or to purify our hearts. God will use others', judgment, discipline, afflictions, defeats, circumstances or His Word and many other vices as He so chooses. Can you see now why purging can be painful? Can you understand why the purging process is referred to as…rending…tearing…refining? We do well to recognize the situations we find ourselves in asking, "Why has God allowed this? What is He trying to show me?" When we ask these questions with a sincere heart, God will answer. A pure heart cannot belong to itself. It must belong to God which brings us to our life changing principle for today…

Principle
A pure heart is a heart that is wholly God's

When we surrender our lives wholly to God upon His holy altar, He accepts it the only way He ever accepted a sacrifice, by turning it into ashes. The fire of God's purging will bring forth from the ashes the rare beauty of Christ and where the beauty of Christ is, there will dwell no unlovely thing. Because a pure heart is a heart that is wholly God's, then…

Benefit
Self finds no glory

We cannot be pure, precious student, and be a reflection of ourselves. Self will never find glory in a pure heart. When a heart is found pure, that heart has found God. Take what we've learned in our time together and meditate upon for a while, beloved. Truth takes time for it is learned a little bit at a time. Let's close out our day by reviewing our memory verse for this week. Write it out below in the space given.

_____

_____

Have I told you today that I love you and I am so proud of you? Well I am beloved…I am. See you on Day Four as we close out our week together.

Day Four

Do you have a heart that longs to be used by God, beloved? Have you ever thought about or desired for God to use you to build His Kingdom, to display His glory to the world? Many of us in Christendom today believe that God could never use us because we are not talented enough, we have nothing to offer God, our past sins are too great, or we are just afraid of what God will ask us to do...the fear of the unknown. If any of these are your thoughts or concerns then I want you to know that I understand. For many years I was plagued with the thought that I was not fit to be used by God. You know what I found to be true? That I am not fit to be used by God! I never will be...not apart from Him. God is fit and if He is dwelling in me and filling me, then there no longer remains room for excuses. God wants to use us for His glory. After all that is why He created us. But how can we make sure that we are a vessel that God can use? What should we be doing to make ourselves available and ready for God to use us? It all revolves around purity, the "blessed" that we have been studying this week. These are questions that we will answer today in our study of God's Word.

If you're ready, let's begin our study. Before you begin, pray that God reveals His truth to you, precious student.

Turn to the end of this week's study and locate Psalm 51:1-17 that we've been looking at for the past few days. According to verse 12, what kind of spirit does David ask God to sustain or give to him?

_____

_____

If you answered, "A free spirit" or as the King James Version says, "a 'free' spirit," then you were correct. Let's see what this word means by turning to our Word Windows Section located in the back of the book. Record what you find in the space provided for you.

Willing

_____

_____

In the light of this meaning, what did David mean when he asked God to renew a "willing" spirit within him? Keep in mind the meaning of this word.

_____

David was asking the God to renew a reputable spirit within him; a spirit that can be used by God, a clean testimony. You see, beloved, because of David's impurities he had marred not only God's name but his reputation with the people of Israel as well. According to verse 13 of this passage, what will David be able to do when God gives him a pure heart?

_____

_____

Have you ever heard the saying: *"I'd rather see a sermon any day than hear one?"* If your reputation outside the Church does not match your walk within the Church, then how will people ever be willing to listen to you when you tell them about Jesus? Why would they want to? This is what David was asking of God. David had blown his testimony with others. David knew that he was ineffective as long as he was impure in the eyes of God. You see, purity is about more than being right in the eyes of God. It's about being a vessel that God can use in the lives of others. Let's look at some other scriptures that show us this truth. Look up the following verses and write out what you learn beside each. Note the promises that God makes to those who are pure; to those who allow purging and refining to take place in their lives.

- **Jeremiah 15:19-21**

_____

_____

_____

- **II Chronicles 16:9**

_____

_____

_____

There is a higher purpose behind the pure heart…it is becoming a vessel fit for the Master's hand. Do you remember the verse we saw in Proverbs 25:4? Let's look at it once more.

Proverbs 25:4

"Take away the dross from the silver, And there comes out a vessel for the smith"

According to this verse, beloved, what kind of vessel is "for" the smith? What kind of vessel does the silver smith desire?

_____

_____

A pure vessel is the vessel that God will and can use. This brings us to our principle for today.

Principle
Purity is God working in you so He can work through you

The silver smith has but one desire and that is to draw out the vessel that He has tested with fire and find it flawless. You see, precious daughter, the vessel represents the skill of the silver smith to all who see it. You are the masterpiece of the Silver Smith. You are His glory…the work of His hands.

An unknown author penned these words long ago…

"But here were only ashes when He came saying,
My daughter, thou hast tried to serve in thine own way,
but now, stretch out thy hands
That I may lead thee out of self's dark cell
And work My will through thee
When Thou has ceased to be."

Turn to the back of your study book and read Matthew 5:13-16. As you read through these verses I want you to draw a circle around every place you see the phrase **"you are"**.

Use any color that you want for this.

There were two places you should have found in this passage. What did we learn from each? See if you can write them out. I've started them for you.

"You are _____

"You are _____

What was Jesus saying to the crowd that day? What is He saying to us? These two phrases are probably some of the most powerful verses regarding the one who is pure. Jesus said that we were the salt of the earth and the light of the world. Salt is a preserver and light is a revealer. We cannot be the salt of the earth and we cannot be the light of the world if we are not pure. If we are not pure, beloved, how will world learn of Jesus and how will the people of the earth be preserved when the He comes?

Because purity is God working in you so He can work through you, then the following will be true…

Benefit
Lives are impacted for the Kingdom of God

Jesus said in John 4:35, **"Behold, I say to you, lift up your eyes and look on the fields, that they are white for harvest.** But where are the laborers that the harvest may be brought in? Where are those who are the salt of the earth and the light of the world? Where is the vessel for the Smith to use? Is it still in the fire, beloved?

Purity within will mean purification without. It means an effective life that can be used by God to reach the world with His message. God is searching for such a woman. Are you that woman, beloved? How I pray that we both will be that woman. Well precious one, as we come to a close of this week's study let's review the principles and benefits that God has revealed to us.

Week in Review

Principle # 1: *A pure heart must be created by God*
Benefit: *A new beginning can be found*

Principle # 2: *A Pure heart comes through refining*
Benefit: *The dross in your life will continue to be removed until God is seen*

Principle #3: *A pure heart is a heart that is wholly God's*
Benefit: *Self finds no glory*

Principle #4: *Purity is God working in you so He can work through you*
Benefit: *Lives are impacted for the kingdom of God*

As always, we will close this week's lesson with a time of personal reflection. Take a few minutes and read through the following questions, beloved, asking God to show you how to apply the truth's that He has shown you this week. God never intended for the seed of truth to fall on rocky soil, but on fertile soil that will take in the seed so it may yield a harvest.

Personal Evaluation

Do you have a rebellious heart toward the things of God?

Are you willing to let God refine you as the silver smith does the silver that you may be pure?

Would you be willing to let God remove the dross that surfaces in your life?

Do you desire to be used by God no matter what it may cost you?

Are there things in your life right now that you know should not be there?

Well, beloved student, one thing is for certain…a pure vessel is a rare find. May you be that rare jewel that radiates the beauty and holiness of God. I am so proud of you for sticking it out this week. You're worked so very hard and I am praying for you as I write this course.

Psalm 51: 1-17

[1]Be gracious to me, O God, according to Your loving kindness; according to the greatness of Your compassion blot out my transgressions.
[2]Wash me thoroughly from my iniquity and cleanse me from my sin.
[3]For I know my transgressions, and my sin is ever before me.
[4]Against You, You only, I have sinned and done what is evil in Your sight, so that You are justified when You speak and blameless when You judge.
[5]Behold I was brought forth in iniquity, and in sin my mother conceived me.
[6]Behold, You desire truth in the innermost being, and in the hidden part You will make me know wisdom.
[7]Purify me with hyssop, and I shall be clean; wash me, and I shall be whiter than snow.

⁸Make me to hear joy and gladness, let the bones which You have broken rejoice.

⁹Hide Your face from my sins and blot out all my iniquities.

¹⁰Create in me a clean heart, O God, and renew a steadfast spirit within me.

¹¹Do not cast me away from Your presence and do not take Your Holy Spirit from me.

¹²Restore to me the joy of Your salvation and sustain me with a willing spirit.

¹³Then I will teach transgressors Your ways, and sinners will be converted to You.

¹⁴Deliver me from bloodguiltiness, O God, the God of my salvation; then my tongue will joyfully sing of Your righteousness.

¹⁵O Lord, open my lips, that my mouth may declare Your praise.

¹⁶For You do not delight in sacrifice, otherwise I would give it; You are not pleased with burnt offering.

¹⁷The sacrifices of God are a broken spirit; a broken and contrite heart, O God, You will not despise.

LESSON SIX
The Blessed Peacemaker

Day One

    Turn on the television on any given day and you find a broadcast on at least one channel reporting about the Middle East. Documentary after documentary flood the airways, the newspapers, the web and the television stations with stories depicting the constant struggle for peace in the Middle East. Many ambassadors from all over the world with noble intentions have been sent by their governments, self interest groups and even some who are self appointed, all with the hopes of being the one who brings peace to a side of the world that is so volatile. The world wide interest in the Middle East is astounding at times, I believe, because the need for peace is of a magnitude that, if it comes, will affect the entire world and future generations. If ever there was a peacemaker needed, it is in this part of the world. They need someone who will eradicate the differences of nations, religious groups and radicals and bring them together to the table of unity.

    Jesus spoke to these people over two thousand years ago because He knew their need for a peacemaker not only in their day, but in days to come. He spoke with such authority, yet with such compassion saying, *"Blessed are the peacemakers for they shall be called sons of God."* Wouldn't you want to be called a child of God, beloved? Wouldn't you want the world to know and see that God is your Father? God is the Father of the blessed peacemaker. The world is in desperate need for the peacemakers to rise up and show themselves strong. Are you a peacemaker, beloved? Are you a child of the living God? What conviction must have fallen upon the hearts of all whose gaze was fixed upon Jesus, for they were listening to the Prince of Peace. Our gaze will be fixed upon the Prince of Peace this week, beloved, as we search to understand what it means to be a blessed Peacemaker. Take time to pray before you begin.

Let's start by reading through Matthew Chapters 5, 6 and 7 that are typed out for you in the back of our study. This passage, the Sermon on the Mount, should be soaking into your memory by now and, prayerfully, you will recall it for years to come. Jesus covers so much in these chapters and we will not be able to cover all of them or even come close to covering them in this study. I do, however, want you to be very familiar with Jesus' entire sermon, not just the *"blesseds"* or *"beatitudes"* as they are often called. Once you've read through these chapters find Matthew 5:7 and write out this *"blessed"* in the space provided for you.

"Blessed are the _____ *, for*

_____ *"*

Before we begin to dig into God's Word and find what it means to be a peacemaker, take a few minutes and write down what you think a peacemaker might be. What do you think their personalities would be like? How would they behave toward others or deal with conflicts?

Turn to your Word Windows Section and find the definition for **"Peacemaker."** Once you've located it, write it out in the space provided for you.

Peacemaker

In its basic meaning as found in the Webster Dictionary, a peacemaker is someone who makes peace. Which brings us to the question…can peace be made and if so, how is it made? I believe for us to find the answers to these questions and for us to fully grasp what a peacemaker is, we must understand what peace is and more importantly, God's heart concerning peace. With this in mind, look up the following verses regarding peace and write out what you learned from each.

- **Psalm 29:11**

- **Psalm 4:8**

- **Psalm 119:165**

- **Isaiah 9:6-7**

- **Isaiah 26:3**

We have looked up the word for **"peacemaker"** as used in Matthew Chapter 5:9. I want us to look at the Hebrew definition for peace as used in the verses we have just looked at from the Old Testament. Turn to your Word Windows Section and find the word **"peace"** and record the meaning in the space provided for you.

Peace

In the light of our word studies, what would you say that a peacemaker is or does?

_____

_____

Look up the following verses in the New Testament and write out what you learned about peace from each.

- **Hebrews 13:20-21**

_____

_____

_____

- **John 14:27**

_____

_____

_____

- **John 16:33**

_____

_____

_____

According to the verses we've looked at so far, beloved, where would you say the source of peace is found?

Before we can ever become a peacemaker, beloved, we must know where the source of peace is. How can we give peace if we do not know where it is found? How can we impart peace if we have never received peace? The difficulty in finding peace comes when we look in places where peace can never be found. The true peacemaker can give peace because he or she has found peace...true peace. The peacemaker knows the principle...that...

Principle
Peace will never be found apart from God

You see, precious student, the peacemaker knows not only that they can find peace in God, but they know that God Himself is peace. He is the one and only source of peace because peace originated from Him. It was initiated by Him and, therefore, it can only come from Him. Any other kind of peace is a false peace and will only bring a false sense of security. If peace does not originate from God then it is not peace and it will not last. There are many this very hour that are searching desperately for peace and will do anything to have, it but the sad thing is they will never find it unless they look to God. Let me show you this in scripture.

I have typed out for you Philippians 4:6-7. Take a minute to read through it.

Philippians 4:6-7

"Be anxious for nothing, but in everything by prayer and supplication with thanksgiving let your requests be made known to God. And the peace of God, which surpasses all comprehension, will guard your hearts and your minds in Christ Jesus".

What can we learn about peace from this verse?

_____

_____

_____

Peace is a guardian for us. In fact, when peace is absent from us we are extremely vulnerable. If the presence of peace is a guardian for our hearts and minds then the absence of peace leaves our hearts and minds unguarded...without protection. Peace is vital to every child of God. When we understand that God is the source of peace and that peace will never be found apart from Him then...

Benefit
Our search for peace is over

Praise the Lord, beloved student that you and I no longer need to search for peace. We know where peace can be found...true peace. Maybe you are at a place in your life where you need for God to impart peace because there is such turmoil and confusion. Times without peace will weary the soul and it will leave the heart battered and defeated. It's during these times of unrest that we become easy prey for the enemy to draw us away from God. The enemy knows that separation from God in any way will take away our peace. It is this separation that must be reconciled before peace can be found. This truth is applicable in any area. This is God's way of keeping us unto Himself.

You see, precious daughter, God is a peacemaker. His heart longs to fill your heart with His peace. His peace passes all comprehension and it is able to guard our minds and our hearts until the very end. As I write this course, I am passing through one of the most difficult times in my life. The storms have been so fierce at times that I thought my heart would surely fail. But just as the winds have howled so mightily, God has been ever so faithful to flood over my heart and soul His abundant and sufficient peace. It's a peace that calms not the storm that we can see in our outward circumstances but the storm that rages within the heart and mind. God's peace whispers, "Peace be still," and the raging ceases. God loves to whisper words of peace to the storm tossed soul because He longs for us to know Him as our blessed peacemaker.

Read the following verse several times. It is our memory verse for this week. May the Lord brand it upon the chambers of your heart.

Memory Verse

John 14: 27

"Peace I leave with you; My peace I give to you; not as the world gives do I give to you. Do not let your heart be troubled, nor let it be fearful."

Day Two

Peace is the most valuable possession that any person, people, group, government, society, church, marriage, business etc. could ever acquire. But for most, peace is only a dream, a pursuit that is often never found. Why is this? Why is peace so difficult for us to not only obtain, but to maintain? Many believe that we should have peace at any cost. Some believe that true peace is impossible in certain circumstances. Others believe that peace is a state of mind and is merely a choice that one must make in order to achieve peace. As we learned yesterday from God's Word, peace is not a choice although it involves choices on our part. It is a resource found only in God. This is the first step to becoming a peacemaker: knowing where your source of peace is found. A peacemaker cannot make peace if he does not possess peace. Learning how to be a peacemaker involves many things, beloved, and we are going to see this in action beginning with our lesson today and continuing throughout the rest of this week.

Pray before you begin, beloved, and ask God to open the eyes of your understanding and to teach you what it means to be a blessed peacemaker.

One of the most powerful stories in the Bible concerning being a peacemaker is found in I Samuel Chapter 25:1-42. It is the story of a woman named Abigail and her dealings with King David. The prophet Samuel has just died and it is a time of mourning for the people of Israel. Take a few moments and turn to the end of this lesson and read through this story to familiarize yourself with it.

There are three main characters in this story. Can you name them? Write out their names below if you have figured out who they are.

- _____

- _____

- _____

These are the three people we will be focusing on the remainder of this week's lesson. Now that you've read through this story, go back through it once more but this time as you do, mark every reference to King David, including any pronouns, by drawing a box around each one with the color of your choosing. By marking these in a distinct way, remember that you are making it easier to go back to those places and glean truth from them. There is much to learn about the life and character of King David just from this one story out of many that are found in the Bible. David was a man after God's own heart and yet he was a man who greatly disappointed God. Although David failed God at times, God still highly exalted David and used him as an example for us even today. God gave David favor with the people of Israel. He was their beloved king that they rejoiced over while he was alive and wept grievously over the day he died. There was never another king like David in the eyes of Israel. So as you mark each reference to David, I want to encourage you to take your time so you don't miss any of them.

What did you learn about Kind David from marking the text?

KING DAVID

_____

_____

_____

THE BLESSED WOMAN

_____

_____

This encounter is filled with powerful truths about being a peacemaker. I don't want us to miss any of them so don't rush your assignments today. Okay beloved? In verse six of this passage David sends a prayer of peace for Nabal. What three things did David pray about for peace concerning Nabal? List them out in the space provided for you. These are so important, beloved, because they set a pattern for our own lives.

Three Areas of Peace

- _____

- _____

- _____

There are three areas of our lives in which the enemy will try to rob us of our peace. They are found here in verse six of this passage and are as follows: our lives, which includes our personal relationship with the Lord, our health, self esteem, forgiveness, just to name a few; households, which includes our relationships with our spouse, children, and other family members; And our belongings, which include our work, our businesses, our wealth, our successes, and our material things.

From what you're read so far, beloved, could you safely say that David's heart was for peace?

_____

How had David treated Nabal concerning his shepherds and herds? Had David done him harm or had he done him good?

_____

_____

Was David ever asked to do the things he did for Nabal or did he choose to do them on his own?

_____

_____

We could say without a shadow of a doubt that David intended no harm for this man but sought his favor with an attitude of peace. David was for peace because if anyone understood what it meant to long for peace it was David. But even though David pursued peace with this man, he did not get peace in return and a situation arose that could have been disastrous if a peacemaker had not intervened. Take a few minutes and read through this story once more to see if you can identify the peacemaker. Record the name of the peacemaker in the space provided for you.

Peacemaker:_____

If you identified the peacemaker as Abigail then you answered correctly. She is the perfect picture of what a true peacemaker is. Take a colored pencil of your choice and go back through our text of study marking every reference to Abigail by drawing a circle around her name. Make sure her color is distinguished from that of David's so the two are easily identified. Once you have finished, record what you gleaned about Abigail by marking the text.

Abigail

_____

_____

_____

THE BLESSED WOMAN

_____

_____

I stand in awe of the spirit of this woman every time I read this account. It's hard to believe that someone in her situation could act with such grace and humility. She truly is the epitome of what a peacemaker is. Typed out below is verse 17 from our passage of study.

I Samuel 25:17

"Now therefore know and consider what you should do, for evil is plotted against our master and against all his household; and he is such a worthless man that no one can speak to him."

According to this verse, what were the two things that the young man told Abigail to do?

"Now therefore _____ and _____."

The young man instructed Abigail to *"know"* and *"consider"* what?

_____

Sometimes, beloved, if we will but stop and "**know**" and "**consider**" what we are to do then we would save ourselves a lot heartache and regrets, wouldn't we? This is what Abigail did. To help us understand what she was doing, turn to your Word Windows Section located in the back of your study book and find the word meanings for these two words. Record your definitions in the spaces provided.

Know

_____
_____
_____
_____
_____
_____

Consider

_____
_____
_____
_____
_____

    What powerful advise this young man gave to Abigail. They were words of life for her that guided her footsteps to make the choices that followed… choices that brought peace.

    Based on these two word meanings, what do you think the young man meant when he advised Abigail to "know" and "consider" what she must do? What was he telling her?

_____
_____

You see, beloved student, when Abigail was told to "know" and "consider" what she must do she was being advised to stop and reflect so she could make a wise decision not based on emotions. When we find ourselves faced with a crisis, a situation that could potentially bring harm to our lives and to the lives of our families, our emotions can often take over and move us to actions that are later regretted. Abigail chose to pause and reflect and draw upon past experiences. She chose to examine herself and the situation. Most of all, she saw an opportunity to grow, an opportunity to intervene for peace. This is what the blessed peacemakers will do. They will make choices based on their knowledge of and experiences with God. A peacemaker does nothing by accident or on a whim of emotions. This brings us to our principle today…this principle is one of the most powerful principles of the peacemaker, but it is also the most difficult.

Principle
A peacemaker is purposeful in action

A peacemaker is purposeful in their choices. They take time to reflect on God and His principles and to remember His heart for peace before they ever take any action or speak a word in a situation. The peacemaker guards his ways to ensure that God is honored and glorified. It's the choice to "know" and "consider" what God would have them do. They examine themselves and they examine the heart and will of God in a situation. They never act in haste or let emotions guide them.

Look up the following scriptures and write out beside each what you learned about God.

- **Psalm 37:23**

- **Proverbs 16:8**

- **Proverbs 3:5-6**

Because the blessed peacemaker is purposeful in the actions they take, then the following is true…

Benefit
Their steps are ordered by the Lord

When we take the time to seek God in a matter and make purposeful choices, we will not lack for direction. We will not wonder what to do, for God will direct every step. He will not let the blessed peacemaker's foot slip. Why? Because the blessed peacemaker shall be called a son of God! A father will not let his son lose his way. Behind every peacemaker is the beating heart of a loving Heavenly Father who watches ever so carefully every step, hearing every word, knowing every thought, and feeling every emotion as His child pursues the path of peace. Remember, beloved, that God is the one who laid out the path of peace for us where there was no path. He blazed out a trail for us to follow. His heart has to be for peace or else He never would have sent Jesus to the cross of Calvary. God is a peacemaker.

Well, precious friend, we will close our time together today by turning back to Day One and reading over our memory verse for this week. Thank you for working so hard today with me. These principles will change your life if you will embrace them whole-heartedly.

See you on Day Three!

Day Three

Have you ever been faced with a situation, a difficulty that you thought could not be resolved? A situation so hopeless that peace was an impossibility? Where peace is absent, then hope is also. With peace comes hope and rest for the soul. Without peace, the heart and soul are at war because the absence of peace means the presence of war. War removes our peace, beloved. You may be living in a home where there is warring every day and peace is nowhere to be found. You may be crying out right this moment, "You just don't know my situation!" I understand, beloved. Peace is the one need of every human soul and sadly, the one most absent. As we continue in our study of the blessed peacemaker I want to encourage you and remind you that we serve a mighty God who is unchanging and immovable. His way is perfect and He works out His plans with perfect faithfulness. Most of all, His heart is for His children…He is on their side!

As always, take a few moments to stop and pray before you begin your study for today.

To understand the depth of what Abigail did, let's look at the character of her husband. Take a few minutes and read through I Samuel 25:1-42 and as you do, mark every reference to Nabal by underlining his name with a colored pencil of your choice. Once you've finished, make a list of everything you learned about this man from marking the text. Remember, it's important to get all of the pronouns as well.

Nabal

_____

_____

_____

_____

From what you've learned so far, would you say that Nabal was a good man or an evil man? Explain why or why not.

_____

_____

_____

What was his reputation with others?

_____

What was his wife's opinion of him? What did she say about him to King David?

_____

_____

It's vital that you understand not only what kind of man he was, but also Abigail's opinion of her husband. You'll understand this as we journey on in our study time together today and more so tomorrow.

In verse 25 of our passage of study Abigail says this regarding her husband:

"Please do not let my lord pay attention to this worthless man, Nabal, for as his name is, so is he. Nabal is his name and folly is with him..."

Abigail said, "As his name is, so is he." In other words, the meaning of his name gave understanding to the kind of man he was. What does his name mean? Let's take a few minutes and find out together. Turn to your Word Windows Section and locate the Hebrew meaning for **"Nabal"** and record it in the space provided for you.

Nabal

_____

_____

To help us understand the gravity of the situation that Abigail was in, turn to I Samuel 25 and read verses 13 & 21. According to these two verses, was David armed for war? What were David's intentions?

_____

_____

Can you even begin to imagine the scene that was playing out? Journey there with me for a moment. Here was one of the most valiant warriors the world had ever seen. He was dressed for battle with four hundred trained warriors behind him who were also dressed and armed for battle! David was to be vindicated and he would not rest until he had brought about due justice. David's intent was to destroy not only Nabal but also all that he owned. There would be no mercy shown. David was coming and with him was death. What an awesome and fearful sight this must have been for those who witnessed it.

We understand that the situation was a grave one and that it seemed pretty hopeless that David would change his mind. Nabal had not shown David respect or compassion although David had protected Nabal's livestock and took care of his shepherds as if they were his own. Now David would show no mercy. Because of the evil deeds of one man, enemies were created, war was birthed and death was eminent. Who would intervene? Who could bring peace into such a hopeless situation? In the midst of all of this, we see emerge before our very eyes the blessed peacemaker. We know her by name: Abigail. Let's look at what Abigail does and in the looking, we will find the true heart of a peacemaker.

Take a few moments and read verses 18-23. According to these verses, what actions did Abigail take to prepare to meet her husband's enemy?

_____

_____

_____

_____

Remembering what David's words were, do you think Abigail was risking her life by what she did? Explain why or why not.

_____

_____

_____

We know that Abigail made purposeful decisions because she considered her ways by pausing and thinking before she acted. We understand from these verses that she chose to be a peacemaker for her husband even though she knew she could be killed. King David was the most powerful man in all the land. He was feared by most and respected as the greatest warrior and most beloved king that had ever reigned. He was a mighty warrior even from childhood. Abigail went out to meet this mighty warrior despite these facts. What courage it took for Abigail to approach an army of 400 who were armed and ready to kill her and her family. Sometimes, beloved, the peacemaker must rise up to face even the fiercest of enemies.

According to verses 23-31 of I Samuel 25, how does Abigail approach King David and what does she say to him?

___

___

___

Where does Abigail put the blame?

___

Does she offer any excuses?

___

Why do you think Abigail did what she did? Was it based on the merits of her husband? What could her motivation have been?

___

___

Abigail is the picture of a true peacemaker. Her heart is for peace, beloved, because she knew that with peace would come life. The blessed peacemaker seeks to preserve life even at the loss of his or her own. She did not place any value on her own life. Why? Because…

Principle
The peacemaker seeks peace in order to preserve life

A peacemaker will seek peace in order to preserve life. It may mean preserving the life of a marriage, a friendship, a job, a wayward child, a ministry, or a reputation. The peacemaker is a preserver of not just physical life, but emotional and spiritual as well. The peacemaker's role is never easy and usually comes with a price. The peacemaker is sacrificial in nature and always places others before their own life or interest. This, beloved, is why the blessed peacemaker is difficult to find. We live in a day where relationships are not valued as a thing of importance or even a necessity, let alone something worth fighting for. Our generation places emphasis on ownership and position. Power and prestige are the grounds for war...the price tags to be paid. This is not so with the one who pursues peace...the one who preserves life.

A peacemaker is a pursuer of peace, beloved. He or she will desire peace above their interests and sometimes their own safety. Abigail did not hesitate to lay herself at the feet of her enemy. She did not hesitate to lay herself on the altar as a sacrifice for peace that life might be preserved. Why is this so, beloved? Because the peacemaker recognizes God's heart concerning peace. It's important that we remember what it means to be a peacemaker.

To help us do this, let's turn to Day One of this week's lesson and review the meaning of what a peacemaker is. Once you've located it, record your answer in the box provided for you. This meaning will come alive for you in a new way after reading the story of Abigail.

A Peacemaker is...

_____

_____

How did Abigail fit this description? What actions did she take that hold true for a peacemaker?

_____

_____

_____

Have you asked yourself the question: "Why did Abigail not expect her husband to go?"

After all, this was his fault…his doing. He was not only a worthless man, but he had brought a death sentence to his entire household, including Abigail. His actions were evil and he should have been the one seeking forgiveness; the one putting himself in harms way. But Abigail never once thought he should go. She never expected him to. Yet she would have had every right, beloved. Here lies the heart of the peacemaker. The peacemaker seeks peace in order to preserve life, but not the life of their own. They consider their life unimportant in the light of peace.

When our motives are to preserve life then…

Benefit
Fear of death is removed

This is not just referring to a physical death, beloved, but also to a death of self, which is usually the most difficult. The peacemaker must die to self before peace can be achieved.

Jesus, in His sermon on the mount, shed light on this truth about the peacemaker. Let's look at these together as we close out our time of study today. Typed out for you is Matthew 5:38-45. I just want us to look over these for now to familiarize ourselves with the truths Jesus gives us in this passage of scripture. Once you've read through them, meditate upon them until tomorrow to give these verses time to settle into your heart and mind. We will look at them more closely tomorrow and line them up with what Abigail did.

Matthew 5:38-45

[38]*You have heard what it was said, "AN EYE FOR AN EYE, AND A TOOTH FOR A TOOTH."*

[39]*"But I say to you, do not resist an evil person; but whoever slaps you on your right cheek, turn the other to him also.*

[40]*"If anyone wants to sue you and take your shirt, let him have your coat also.*

[41]*"Whoever forces you to go one mile, go with him two."*

[42]"Give to him who asks of you, and do not turn away from him who wants to borrow from you.
[43]"You have heard that it was said, 'YOU SHALL LOVE YOUR NEIGHBOR AND HATE YOUR ENEMY."
[44]"But I say to you, love your enemies and pray for those who persecute you,
[45]"So that you may be sons of your Father who is in heaven. For He causes His sun to rise on the evil and the good, and sends rain on the righteous and the unrighteous."

Review your memory verse, beloved, and I will see you on Day Four! Thank you for working so diligently today. We are learning the role of the peacemaker is not easy but what a beautiful reward there is waiting for the one who chooses it.

Day Four

Do you consider yourself to be a peacemaker, beloved? Have you ever been put into a situation where you had to take on the role of a peacemaker? If so, then I'm sure you would agree you found yourself in a most difficult situation. As we have been studying in this week's lesson, the role of the peacemaker involves many parts. Parts we may not fully understand this side of heaven, but parts nonetheless that God has established. I want us to continue to look at the life of Abigail and how she became one of the greatest peacemaker's in the Bible. Take time to pray, precious student, before you begin today's lesson.

Let's begin our study time today by reading through the account of Abigail in I Samuel 25 that we've been studying thus far this week. Remember that repetition brings recollection. We want to remember God's Word and hide it in our hearts and there is no better way to do that than to read and re-read the text over and over again. It takes time for God's Word to sink into our hearts and saturate our minds. I believe that God made our hearts and minds like sponges to soak up His truths. Let's soak them up today.

According to I Samuel 25:24, what did Abigail say to Kind David when she fell at his feet? There were three things she said to him when she fell down before him.

1._____

2._____

3._____

How powerful are the words: *"On me alone, my lord, be the blame."* She made no excuses regarding her husband. She gave no detailed story of how difficult it was to be married to such an evil man nor did she allow the blame to fall on her husband where it should have rightfully fallen. The moment that she spoke these words, Abigail offered herself in place of her husband. Her concern was not for justice or she would have offered her husband and not herself. Her primary objective was making peace…making the wrong right.

It's important to note in this verse how Abigail refers to herself in the presence of King David. She calls herself his "maidservant"." The King James Version uses the word, "handmaid." Turn your Word Windows Section and find the meaning of **"Maidservant"** and record it in the space provided for you.

Maidservant

Based on the meaning of this word and her use of it, what does this tell us about Abigail's spirit? What was her attitude as she approached David?

_____

_____

This blessed peacemaker had a spirit of humility…a spirit that was completely surrendered of all rights. She was not there to represent herself or even her husband. She was there representing the rights of and acknowledging the rights of David, who was the enemy. This is a powerful truth, beloved, if we will grab hold of it. The blessed peacemaker must surrender all rights, all privileges, all honor, all dignity, and all innocence. We live in a society where everyone is taught and encouraged to exercise their rights. To be taught to surrender one's rights is unheard of. Yet this is the role of the peacemaker. A peacemaker cannot make peace with his enemies if he insists on exercising his rights. You cannot have any rights as a peacemaker. This is a hard truth, beloved, but nevertheless, it is truth.

No one demonstrated this more than the Lord Jesus. The greatest peacemaker of all time teaching this truth knew and understood the cost, the sacrifice for being a peacemaker. Let's look at this together. Look up the following verses and record what you learned about the Lord Jesus out beside each.

- **Philippians 2:5-8**

_____

_____

_____

- **Matthew 20:28**

_____

_____

_____

- **John 13:12-16**

_____

_____

_____

Did Jesus have an attitude of a servant, beloved? Did He have the heart of a peacemaker? Explain why or why not.

_____

_____

The story of Abigail is much more than a story. It is a portrait of what Jesus has done for us, beloved. The story of our lives is woven beautifully in that of Abigail's: the innocent taking on the guilt of the guilty. Do you see the likeness, beloved? To help us see this, look up the following verses and record what you learn from each. Take your time as you read each passage for they are rich in truth. When viewed in the light of the story of the blessed peacemaker, Abigail, they take on life before us. I pray that you will understand these wonderful truths about your salvation in a new and more meaningful way as never before.

- **Ephesians 3:13-17**

_____

_____

_____

- **Romans 5: 1-10**

_____

_____

_____

- **Colossians 1:19-22**

_____

_____

_____

Can you see how Jesus was a peacemaker? Can you see how he took on the role of the one who brings peace between God and man…between God and you, beloved student? Let us look at one more beautiful act in the life of Abigail that also points us to Jesus. Do you remember what Abigail did first, beloved? To help you remember, go back to I Samuel 25 and read what Abigail did when she heard what had happened. She gathered her offering. What did she do with that offering once it was prepared?

_____

If you answered that she sent it on ahead of her then you answered correctly, beloved student. Why did she do this? Why did she not take the peace offerings with her? Why did she send it on before her? To help us understand this, read the passage of scriptures from Hebrews typed out for you and note what Jesus did.

Hebrews 6: 19-20

[19] *"This hope we have as an anchor of the soul, a hope both sure and steadfast and one which enters within the veil,*
[20] *"where Jesus has entered as a forerunner for us..."*

Hebrews 9:11,12 & 24

[11] *"But when Christ appeared as a high priest of the good things to come, He entered through the greater and more perfect tabernacle, not made with hands, that is to say, not of this creation;*
[12] *"and not through the blood of goats and calves, but through His own blood, He entered the holy place once for all, having obtained eternal redemption."*
[24] *"For Christ did not enter a holy place made with hands, a mere copy of the true one, but into heaven itself, now to appear in the presence of God for us.*

When Abigail sent her men ahead with the gifts she had prepared, she was sending them as a forerunner. The forerunner soothes the wrath of the enemy to prepare a way for peace to be made. This is what Jesus did for us, beloved. He went as a forerunner and His offering soothed the wrath of God that He had toward us. If David had been unwilling to accept Abigail's offering of peace then death would have come. Her offering was acceptable before the King. This is the role of a peacemaker. This brings us to our truth today. A peacemaker...

Principle
Presents an acceptable offering

Sometimes, beloved, when we take on the role of a peacemaker in our own lives, we must send a forerunner ahead of us before peace can be made.

Prayer is the most powerful forerunner because it moves the heart of God. Which then moves the heart of man. There will be times when we will have to face the most difficult of people in hopes of obtaining peace. This is when it is vital that you allow the blessed Holy Spirit to go before you to prepare the way. When He has gone before us then peace will follow. A verse that says this is: Proverbs 16:7:

"When a man's ways are pleasing to the Lord, He makes even his enemies to be at peace with him."

Our forerunner can come in many different shapes and sizes. It can mean our character in the midst of a situation, our attitude, our prayers, our motives and a host many other things. God always sends a forerunner before He works in the heart of man. God always prepares the ground He intends to plant and harvest. Even Jesus had a forerunner. His name was John the Baptist. So even Jesus, who was a forerunner for us, had a voice crying, "Prepare ye the way of the Lord."

Jesus was not only our forerunner, He was our offering of peace to God. He presented Himself to the Father and His wrath was satisfied, bringing peace between God and man once again.

Isaiah 9:6-7 says...

⁶"For a child will be born to us, a son will be given to us; And the government will rest on His shoulders; And His name will be called Wonderful Counselor, Mighty God, Eternal Father, Prince of Peace.
⁷"There will be no end to the increase of His government or of peace, on the throne of David and over his kingdom, to establish it and to uphold it with justice and righteousness from then on and forevermore. The zeal of the Lord of hosts will accomplish this."

Did you catch the ending part, beloved? "The zeal of the Lord of hosts will accomplish this." Remember God is for peace. It was His zeal, His heart that brought about Calvary in order to make peace between you and Him. You can be at peace with God no matter what if you have the blessed peacemaker Himself; the Lord Jesus Christ. Because when an acceptable offering is made then...

Benefit
Enmity is gone

There would arise a peacemaker, beloved, from the very lineage of King David and there will be no end to His government of peace. Take a minute and record this "blessedness" on your chart in the back of your book. "Blessed are the peacemakers, for they shall be called sons of God."

Let's review the principles and benefits of the blessed peacemaker that we've learned this week.

Week in Review

Principle # 1: *Peace will never be found apart from God*
Benefit: *Our search for peace is over*

Principle # 2: *Purposeful in action*
Benefit: *Their steps are ordered by the Lord*

Principle #3: *Seeks peace in order to preserve life*
Benefit: *Fear of death is removed*

Principle #4: *Presents an acceptable offering*
Benefit: *Enmity is gone*

We've learned some powerful truths this week about the peacemaker, haven't we? How do these precious truths apply to our every day lives, beloved? Let's pause for a time of personal reflection and challenge. Read through the following questions and let them have time to rest upon the ears of your heart. Ask God to search you and try you to the deepest part of your being.

Personal Evaluation

Do you have a heart for peace?

Is there someone in your life right now that you are not at peace with? If so, have you been the "blessed peacemaker" that Abigail was in this situation?

Are you willing to take someone's blame in order to bring peace?

Do you understand what Jesus did for you so you and God could be a peace with one another?

Did Jesus ever ask you to go and meet your enemy, or did He just gladly go for you, even though you were the one who had brought death to your life?

That last question just rips at my heart, beloved. Just as Abigail never asked her husband to go out and face the enemy who was coming to take his life, neither did Jesus ask you to go and face God concerning the sins you had committed. What a blessed peacemaker we have precious daughter, that you are. How He loved you when stepped out into your place and fell on His face before the Father, the righteous judge and said: *"On me alone, Father, be all the blame."*

Let's close our week together on our knees before our beloved peacemaker thanking Him and loving Him for all He has done. Who can measure how high, how wide, how long, and how deep the Savior's love is for us.

Much love for you, precious student. Hang in there; only two more weeks to go!

THE BLESSED WOMAN

I Samuel 25:1-42

¹Then Samuel died; and all Israel gathered together and mourned for him, and buried him at his house in Ramah And David arose and went down to the wilderness of Paran.

²Now there was a man in Maon whose business was in Carmel; and the man was very rich, and he had three thousand sheep and a thousand goats. And it came about while he was shearing his sheep in Carmel

³(now the man's name was Nabal, and his wife's name was Abigail. And the woman was intelligent and beautiful in appearance, but the man was harsh and evil in his dealings, and he was a Calebite),

⁴that David heard in the wilderness that Nabal was shearing his sheep.

⁵So David sent ten young men; and David said to the young men, "Go up to Carmel, visit Nabal and greet him in my name;

⁶and thus you shall say, 'Have a long life, peace be to you, and peace be to your house, and peace be to all that you have.

⁷'Now I have heard that you have shearers; now your shepherds have been with us and we have not insulted them, nor have they missed anything all the days they were in Carmel.

⁸'Ask your young men and they will tell you. Therefore let my young men find favor in your eyes, for we have come on a festive day. Please give whatever you find at hand to your servants and to your son David.'"

⁹When David's young men came, they spoke to Nabal according to all these words in David's name; then they waited.

¹⁰But Nabal answered David's servants and said, "Who is David? And who is the son of Jesse? There are many servants today who are each breaking away from his master.

¹¹"Shall I then take my bread and my water and my meat that I have slaughtered for my shearers, and give it to men whose origin I do not know?"

¹²So David's young men retraced their way and went back; and they came and told him according to all these words.

¹³David said to his men, "Each of you gird on his sword." So each man girded on his sword. And David also girded on his sword, and about four hundred men went up behind David while two hundred stayed with the baggage.

[14]But one of the young men told Abigail, Nabal's wife, saying, "Behold, David sent messengers from the wilderness to greet our master, and he scorned them.

[15]"Yet the men were very good to us, and we were not insulted, nor did we miss anything as long as we went about with them, while we were in the fields.

[16]"They were a wall to us both by night and by day, all the time we were with them tending the sheep.

[17]"Now therefore, know and consider what you should do, for evil is plotted against our master and against all his household; and he is such a worthless man that no one can speak to him."

[18]Then Abigail hurried and took two hundred loaves of bread and two jugs of wine and five sheep already prepared and five measures of roasted grain and a hundred clusters of raisins and two hundred cakes of figs, and loaded them on donkeys.

[19]She said to her young men, "Go on before me; behold, I am coming after you." But she did not tell her husband Nabal.

[20]It came about as she was riding on her donkey and coming down by the hidden part of the mountain, that behold, David and his men were coming down toward her; so she met them.

[21]Now David had said, "Surely in vain I have guarded all that this man has in the wilderness, so that nothing was missed of all that belonged to him; and he has returned me evil for good.

[22]"May God do so to the enemies of David, and more also, if by morning I leave as much as one male of any who belong to him."

[23]When Abigail saw David, she hurried and dismounted from her donkey, and fell on her face before David and bowed herself to the ground.

[24]She fell at his feet and said, "On me alone, my lord, be the blame. And please let your maidservant speak to you, and listen to the words of your maidservant.

[25]"Please do not let my lord pay attention to this worthless man, Nabal, for as his name is, so is he. Nabal is his name and folly is with him; but I your maidservant did not see the young men of my lord whom you sent.

[26]"Now therefore, my lord, as the LORD lives, and as your soul lives, since the LORD has restrained you from shedding blood, and from avenging yourself by your own hand, now then let your enemies and those who seek evil against my lord, be as Nabal.

THE BLESSED WOMAN

²⁷"Now let this gift which your maidservant has brought to my lord be given to the young men who accompany my lord.

²⁸"Please forgive the transgression of your maidservant; for the LORD will certainly make for my lord an enduring house, because my lord is fighting the battles of the LORD, and evil will not be found in you all your days.

²⁹"Should anyone rise up to pursue you and to seek your life, then the life of my lord shall be bound in the bundle of the living with the LORD your God; but the lives of your enemies He will sling out as from the hollow of a sling.

³⁰"And when the LORD does for my lord according to all the good that He has spoken concerning you, and appoints you ruler over Israel,

³¹this will not cause grief or a troubled heart to my lord, both by having shed blood without cause and by my lord having avenged himself. When the LORD deals well with my lord, then remember your maidservant."

³²Then David said to Abigail, "Blessed be the LORD God of Israel, who sent you this day to meet me,

³³and blessed be your discernment, and blessed be you, who have kept me this day from bloodshed and from avenging myself by my own hand.

³⁴"Nevertheless, as the LORD God of Israel lives, who has restrained me from harming you, unless you had come quickly to meet me, surely there would not have been left to Nabal until the morning light as much as one male."

³⁵So David received from her hand what she had brought him and said to her, "Go up to your house in peace. See, I have listened to you and granted your request."

³⁶Then Abigail came to Nabal, and behold, he was holding a feast in his house, like the feast of a king. And Nabal's heart was merry within him, for he was very drunk; so she did not tell him anything at all until the morning light.

³⁷But in the morning, when the wine had gone out of Nabal, his wife told him these things, and his heart died within him so that he became as a stone.

³⁸About ten days later, the LORD struck Nabal and he died.

³⁹When David heard that Nabal was dead, he said, "Blessed be the LORD, who has pleaded the cause of my reproach from the hand of Nabal and has kept back His servant from evil. The LORD has also returned the evildoing of Nabal on his own head." Then David sent a proposal to Abigail, to take her as his wife.

⁴⁰When the servants of David came to Abigail at Carmel, they spoke to her, saying, "David has sent us to you to take you as his wife."

[41] She arose and bowed with her face to the ground and said, "Behold, your maidservant is a maid to wash the feet of my lord's servants."

[42] Then Abigail quickly arose, and rode on a donkey, with her five maidens who attended her; and she followed the messengers of David and became his wife.

LESSON SEVEN
Salt and Light

Day One

Have you ever wondered how Jesus refers to you when He speaks of you to the Father? Does He call you by name? Does He refer to you by country, by age, or maybe even by church? Does He call you by ministry or gifts? Does He refer to you as friend, daughter, or even Christian? If those belonging to the world were to ask Jesus about you, what would He say to them? How would He describe you to the people of the world? What are you to be, beloved, and what are you to do? How will what you do reflect what you are? We will journey together to find the answers and oh the power it can have in our lives if we will take hold of what the Lord will show to us today through the study of His Word on the Sermon on the Mount.

Take time to pray, precious student, and ask the Lord to reveal truth in your innermost being. He alone contains all knowledge. All wisdom and understanding comes from Him. Ask Him to transform you through the power of His Word.

If you are ready to get started…then let's go. To help the Sermon on the Mount soak deeper into our hearts, let's begin our study time together by reading through Matthew Chapters 5, 6, and 7. Once you finished, meet me back here.

In Matthew 5:13 and 14 Jesus uses two words to describe those who belong to the Kingdom of God. I have typed out these two verses for you. Read through them and underline the phrase: "You are" with the color of your choosing.

Matthew 5:13 & 14

[13] *"You are the salt of the earth: but if the salt has become tasteless, how can it be made salty again? It is no longer good for anything, except to be thrown out and trampled under foot by men.*
[14] *"You are the light of the world. A city set on a hill cannot be hidden..."*

There were two things Jesus called those who belonged to the Kingdom of God. Did you find them both? If so, see if you can fill in the blanks.

"You are the _____

"You are the _____

Jesus said that we were the salt of the earth and the light of the world. Two powerful adjectives! Let's look at the first one: salt. What does it mean to be the salt of the earth? I know this may sound silly, beloved, but indulge me for just a moment. Jesus did not tell us that we were the salt of the ocean, or of the mines, or even of the food! Jesus wasn't talking about ordinary salt like you and I know. He told us that we were the salt of the earth, but what does it mean to be the salt of the earth? To help us, beloved, let's look up some verses that use the word 'salt' in the Old and New Testaments. Record what you learned about salt beside each verse.

- **Leviticus 2:13**

_____

_____

_____

THE BLESSED WOMAN

- **Numbers 18:19**

_____

_____

_____

- **Colossians 4:6**

_____

_____

_____

- **Ezekiel 43: 22-24**

_____

_____

_____

- **Job 6:6**

_____

_____

_____

Turn to your Word Windows Section and look up the definition for the word **"salt"** as used in the verses we have looked at and the one Jesus used in His Sermon on the Mount. Record your findings in the space provided.

Salt

_____

_____

Salt was used in a variety of ways. In Ancient Rome it was used as wages for the Soldiers. Can you imagine being paid in salt, beloved? Salt in Biblical times was much different than that of the salt we use today. Our salt is refined and pure and long ago it wasn't. Because salt in Biblical times came in varying degrees of purity it was used for many different things. It was used to season food, adding flavor when necessary. It was used as an antiseptic for killing bacteria and as a preservative to halt the spread of decay. Impure salt was often mixed into the soil as a fertilizer or to help in decomposition. The danger of mixing it into the soil was that if too much was used, it would ruin the minerals in the soil leaving it sterile and useless for harvesting. In the book of Judges we see that when a city was conquered the enemy would sow that city with salt as a sign of its complete and eternal ruin. The poorest quality of salt was used to make paths for people to tread upon because it was good for nothing else.

Look up the following verses that are beautiful cross-references for Matthew 5:13 and record what you learned about salt from each.

- **Luke 14:33-35**

_____

_____

_____

- **Mark 9:50**

_____

_____

_____

Jesus was showing us our purpose for living…our reason for existence upon the earth. You see, beloved, being a Christian is not about what you do but rather it's about what you are. What you are will determine what you do. If salt is present and if it is pure salt, then it makes a difference. It preserves life, it adds flavor, it changes things and makes them better. Salt halts corruption. Out of all of these there is one more thing that salt does that I believe is a very powerful characteristic: it causes thirst. Do you cause others to thirst for the fountain of living water?

Salt has many different uses, doesn't it, beloved? It can be a very powerful tool when used correctly: it has the power to stop decay and promote life; it has the power to purify and to enhance flavor, just to name a few. Even though it is a most precious commodity, there is one thing that must be present before even the purest of salt can useful…

Principle
Salt must be poured out

Even the purest salt is no good until it is poured out. If you bottled it up, it would not matter how tasteful or useful it was if you never opened up the bottle and poured it out. It was never meant to be kept locked away. It was designed to be poured out upon the earth. When this takes place powerful things can happen. The perfect example of the power of salt is given in II Kings 2:19-22. Take a few minutes to read through these verses that are typed out for you, and then answer the question that follows.

II Kings 2:19-22

[19] *"Then the men of the city said to Elisha, "Behold now, the situation of this city is pleasant, as my lord sees; but the water is bad and the land is unfruitful."*

[20] *He said, "Bring me a new jar, and put salt in it." So they brought it to him.*

[21] *He went out to the spring of water and threw salt in it and said, "Thus says the LORD, 'I have purified these waters; there shall not be from there death or unfruitfulness any longer.'"*

²²*So the waters have been purified to this day, according to the word of Elisha which he spoke.*

According to these verses, what change did the salt bring about in the waters?

_____

_____

The power of salt! Do you see it, beloved? This is what you are to be…salt to the earth. When salt is poured out…

Benefit
It becomes a powerful force upon the earth

Where there is salt, death cannot prevail. A life that is salty will have the power to defeat spiritual death and impart eternal life. Do you cause others to thirst for the Living Waters of Jesus? Do you make a difference in the world around you? When salt is on the scene its presence cannot be hidden because salt changes its environment. Salt, when it is poured out, is a powerful force upon the earth…in the lives of others. Let these truths that we have learned today have time to penetrate to the deepest level of your being.

Our memory verse for this week is Mark 9:50. We've already looked at it today. It is typed out for you. Take a few minutes to read over it several times to familiarize yourself so memorization will come faster.

Memory Verse

Mark 9:50

"Salt is good; but if the salt becomes un-salty, with what will you make it salty again? Have salt in yourselves, and be at peace with one another."

Well, my precious friend, you have worked so hard today in your study. Being salt is not easy, is it? But being salt is powerful in the hands of God! Will you be that salt in His hands? I am stopping right now and I am bowing my knees in prayer for you, my friend, who will come to this place one day long after I have written this page. Know that when you get to this place that this writer has prayed for you. You are in my thoughts right now, beloved. The date is October 17, 2006 and it is about the midnight hour. May you feel God's presence in a special way and know that He is beckoning you to be salt…to be salt that is poured out upon the earth.

Remember, that it is not what we do, but it is what we are that will bring about change in the world.

Much love to you…I will see you on Day Two.

Day Two

We learned on Day One of our study this week that we are to be salt and light. Jesus spoke these words to His followers long ago up on a hillside. What strange words this man, who claimed to be the Son of God, was speaking. He had been known to speak strange things before but His words were very different and I'm sure they raised a lot of questions. Could you imagine being told that you are the salt of the earth, or the light of the world? How can you and I be salt? How can you and I be light? Don't you know that these words were pondered over and over again in the minds of those who heard that day? I imagine there were many who lost sleep that night after sitting at the feet of Jesus, being confronted with such powerfully convicting words. Words never spoken before.

If someone came up and asked you the question: "Hey, are you salty?" What would you think? How would you respond? This is what we are going to continue looking at today during our study time together. Take time to pray, precious student, before you begin. Every great work starts with prayer.

Turn to Matthew 5:13 and, using the scripture, fill in the words in the space provided for you.

Matthew 5:13

You _____ the _____ of the _____; but if the salt has become _____, how can it be _____ salty again?
    It is no longer _____ for anything, except to be _____
    Out and _____ underfoot by _____.

Take a colored pencil of your choice and mark every reference to the word **"Salt,"** including all pronouns, by drawing a circle around each. Once you've finished, make a list of everything you learned about salt by marking the passage.

Salt

_____

_____

_____

Did Jesus say when we would become salt?

_____

What is the second word used in this verse?

_____

He did not say that you are to be the salt of the earth. He said you **ARE** the salt of the earth. What do you think Jesus meant when He said this?

_____

_____

Jesus did not command the people to become salt or even give them a character list of what to do to become salt. Jesus was not speaking of a futuristic occurrence, or a goal to strive for, but rather He was making a statement of a present condition. Jesus looked out into the crowd that day and spoke very factually saying: "You are the salt of the earth." Do you consider yourself to be salt, beloved? Jesus does.

I have heard teaching on the Sermon on the Mount many times during my Christian life, including this portion on the salt of the earth. I heard the question asked during the application of this truth: "Are you salt"? This always challenged me when I heard it and caused me to look inward and consider my own life. One day, while studying this passage, the Holy Spirit revealed to me that Jesus never asked that question when He was teaching on this subject. He never did. He simply stated that we are the salt of the earth. This should tell us that we were created to be salt…redeemed to be salt…commanded that we are salt.

Being salt or becoming salt is not an option that we were given nor will we ever be given.

We aren't to be salt only when we are in a right relationship with the Lord, or only when our circumstances are springing up roses everywhere; when our children are good; when our marriages are wonderful; when our jobs are perfect; when we are in a Church service; or only if we are on a mission field somewhere. Jesus looked at you, beloved, and said: "You are the salt of the earth." One of the greatest responsibilities we have is found right here in this truth.

So the question should not be: **"Are you salt?"** The question should be: **"What kind of salt are you?"** We learned in our study time yesterday that there are varying kinds of salt. Make a list of what salt was, and can be, used for as we learned from Day One.

Uses of Salt

_____

_____

_____

Jesus gave us a hint of what our problem would be with this truth in the words that followed His powerful declaration in Matthew 5:13. Let us look at them together.

"You are the salt of the earth; but if the salt has become tasteless, how can it be made salty again? It is no longer good for anything, except to be thrown out and trampled under foot by men."

According to this verse, what kind of salt do you think Jesus desires for us to be?

_____

Jesus told His listeners that when salt changes…when it becomes something it was never intended to be, then it loses its worth or its usefulness and it never fulfills the purpose for which it was created. This brings us to our principle today…

Principle
Salt is to remain pure

According to Matthew 5:13, what did Jesus say the salt was good for once it lost its saltiness? There were two things.

1._____

2._____

You see, precious student, when salt is not pure one of two things will happen to it. It will be thrown away as invaluable and others will trample it upon. Salt will not only lose its effectiveness, it will lose the respect of others. Others will place no value in it because to them it is worthless.

If we are the salt of the earth, beloved, then can this also happen to us if we lose our saltiness?

Just as salt is to be pure in order to be useable or effective, then so are we to be pure. Like salt, the purer we are the more powerful and valuable we become. When we lose our purity, when sin enters into our lives, then we, like salt, cannot be used and others will not want what we have. The name of the Lord will have no weight out in the world and the world will mock it by trampling His name underfoot. When this happens, precious student, how will we ever go make what is wrong right? Once a testimony is lost, once the saltiness is lost, how can it be regained? Jesus knew that this was nearly an impossibility. Do you see the importance, beloved, of pure salt? Salt must be pure…and when it is pure…

Benefit
It will accomplish the Lord's purpose

So, beloved, again the question is not: "Are you salt?" but rather, "What kind of salt are you?" Are you a life that is useful and effective in the world? Does your life stop corruption? Does it promote life…eternal life? Does it cause others to thirst for Jesus? Are you pure or have you allowed sin in to such a degree that you have lost your testimony with others? What is your salt worth? You can measure it by the impact you are making in the lives of those around you.

I know these are difficult questions, beloved…I understand. I, too, have had to face these before I could ever write them for you. The good news is, beloved, that we can become pure again! We can filter out the unholy things and characteristics and become salt that is useful…salt that has worth because it is powerful. You are the salt of the earth, precious student…what kind of salt will you choose to be?

As we close our time together, I want to challenge you to get on your knees with the Lord and ask Him to search your heart and see if there be any hurtful way in you. Confess these things as sin. According to I John 1:9, when you confess your sins before Him, He is faithful and just to forgive you of them. As He reveals them to you, beloved, why don't you take a few minutes to write them down? This is a powerful tool for cleansing our lives. The question to ask yourself is: What are the impurities in my life that I must remove in order to be salty again? I understand that this is difficult but I strongly encourage you to take the time to do this.

I have provided space for you.

Impurities that I must remove from my life

_____

_____

_____

Let me share with you Matthew 5:13 as translated by the Amplified Bible.

"You are the salt of the earth, but if salt has lost its taste (its strength, its quality), how can its saltiness be restored? It is not good for anything any longer but to be thrown out and trodden underfoot by men."

Sin in our lives saps our strength and maligns the quality of Christian that we ought to be. The world will see no value in us…nothing that they will want or thirst for. The name of God will have no respect by the men of the earth because the salt is useless and deemed unimportant…the lowest of the low. Is it any wonder the names of God and Jesus are used as profanity with absolutely no thought or fear? There is no respect for God and no fear of Him before the eyes of man. Why? Because the earth does not have the salt that it so desperately needs. May we be the pure salt and may we pour out our lives upon the earth that Jesus loved so much that He gave His life for.

Thank you for your effort to become what God wants you to be. I pray that you and I will be the salt He intends for us to be. Truth, is sometimes hard and truth takes time to embrace and integrate it into our everyday lives. We must meditate upon truth as we continuously apply it to our lives. When this happens in our lives then a learned truth becomes a living truth for the world to see. God's Word will not return void because He watches over His Word to perform it…to bring it to pass…to give life to it (Jeremiah 1:12).

Love to you, precious student. I am so proud of you.

Day Three

Have you ever met, or do you know someone, who just seems to light up a room when they walk in it; a person who is so vibrant, so radiant that your heart smiles at just the thought of them; someone whose smile is contagious…someone whose eyes sparkle because they are overflowing with the joy that is within them? Don't you just love to meet people like this, beloved? They just bring an added joy to your steps when your path crosses with theirs. You usually never forget these kinds of people and when you leave their presence you are a better person having been in it.

Have you ever been in a person's presence that was completely the opposite of this? In fact, their presence not only did not radiate joy, but darkness and gloom seemed to be their very adornment? Have you ever walked away from someone who was so negative and unhappy that you felt worse having been in their presence even for a short while; people who never smile; who seem to have no reason for living day after day? God has allowed me to meet women all over the world and wherever He sends me, there is always a mixture of those who exuberate light and then those who are veiled in darkness, without hope and joy in their lives. In fact, I know a woman who, in all the years I have known her, I have never once seen her smile.

There are definitely those who are lights in the world, but there are, without doubt, those who are not. Today and tomorrow I want us to look at what it means to be the "light of the world." After all, these are the words of Jesus spoken so long ago and written down for us to light our way. Before you begin, remember to pray asking God to open the eyes of your understanding that you may behold wonderful truths from His Word.

Let's begin today by reading through our three chapters of Matthew that, by now, we are becoming so familiar with. Once you've finished I want us to focus our attention on Matthew 5:14-16. Turn to the back of your book and locate Matthew Chapters 5, 6, and 7 which are typed out for you and read through just these three verses in Chapter 5. As you do, take a yellow colored pencil and mark every reference to the word **"light"** by drawing a cloud type symbol around each. Make sure you get every pronoun referring to **"light"** as well. I don't want you to miss any of them.

According to these verses and your markings, what did you learn by marking the word **"light?"**

Light

Look up the following verses for **"light"** and record out beside each what you learned.

- **Genesis 1:3-4**

- **Psalm 27:1**

- **Micah 7:8**

_____

_____

_____

- **I John 1:5-7**

_____

_____

_____

- **II Corinthians 6:14**

_____

_____

_____

Beloved, where does light come from? Where did it originate from?

_____

We have looked at just a few verses on "light" in the Old and New Testament. There are many, beloved, and we can't begin to touch them all during the course of this week's lesson. But to help us get a better handle on what the word "light" means, turn to your Word Windows Section and find the Hebrew and Greek definitions for the word **"light."** There is space provided for you for both of these. In Lesson Two of this study we looked at the New Testament word for "light" as used in Matthew 5, but I want us to revisit this word meaning in light of the scriptures we have looked at today. Okay beloved? So, if this word seems familiar this is why.

Light (as used in the Old Testament)

_____

_____

_____

Light (as used in the New Testament)

_____

_____

_____

From the scriptures we have looked at so far and the word definitions, what do you think Jesus meant when He said: *"You are the light of the world?"* In your own words, how would you describe this life?

_____

_____

_____

Beloved, did Jesus say we were to become light or that we are light?

_____

Just like salt, light is not something we become at a future date or are becoming, but rather we ARE light according to Jesus. Fill in the words below to finish the scripture.

Matthew 5:14-16

"You _____ the light of the _____. A _____ set on a _____ cannot be _____; nor does anyone light a _____ and put it under a basket, but on the lampstand, and it gives _____ to _____ who are in the _____. Let your light _____ before _____ in such a way that they may _____ your good works, and _____ your _____ Who is in heaven."

Jesus gave us a standard to measure whether or not our light was shinning in such a way that it was meant to shine. According to Jesus, if our light is shining in this way, what will men do when they see it?

_____

What were we not do to with our light?

_____

Jesus said that no light is to be put under a table…it's not to be hidden. So this tells us that

Principle
Light is to be seen

Light was never meant to be hidden. This is why God gave us light first when He created the heavens and the earth. Did you realize, beloved, that we are never without light in our world, even when it is night? God wanted to so remind us of this truth that He hung the moon and the sun for us to see everyday of our lives. God never intended for His world to be in darkness.

According to Jesus' words in Matthew 5:16, when the world sees our light they glorify God because of it. For them to glorify God, where must their focus be?

_____

That's right, beloved...on God. This is the power of light in the world. It illuminates who God is. Light is revealing because it reveals what is hidden by the darkness. There are many this hour that do not know of the deep love of God nor do they know of His son, Jesus Christ. God desires for all to know Him and so He put His light within the heart of all those who belong to Him in order to light the way for others to find Him.

Do you see, it beloved? Light is to be seen so that...

Benefit
What is hidden in the darkness will be revealed

No verse better shows this truth than Isaiah 9:2 which says... *"The people who walk in darkness will see a great light; those who live in a dark land, the light will shine on them."*

When light comes, beloved, darkness flees, for darkness cannot remain in the presence of light.

There are thousands who die daily, precious student, never having found their way out of the darkness because there was no light to show them the way. Do you desire to be the blessed woman? Then let your light shine before others in such a way that they may see your good works and glorify the Father! Be that light that blazes a trail for others to follow.

Do you remember the day that you saw the light? Aren't you glad that God did not leave you in the darkness? He could have, precious, and He would have had every right to, but because He loved us so, He sent the Light of the world that whosoever would believe in Him would not perish, but have everlasting life. Will you take time to close our time together thanking God for sending the Light that called you out of darkness...that Light that beckoned you, "Come hither for this is the pathway to the Living God."

We have one more day together this week, beloved student. Hang in there until the end. I am ever so thankful for you. You have journeyed this far and to God be the glory.

Day Four

People who change their world are lights in a dark world. Jesus said in Matthew 5:14, *"You are the light of the world, a city set on a hill."* Did you know that light is one of the most powerful forces in the universe? It governs our day and it illuminates our night skies. Our galaxy is just one of billions, and what makes it so beautiful is the splendor of the heavenly host that illuminates the space it occupies. These lights are so powerful and so radiant that surely it would be fitting to describe them as the lights of the world! There are so many of them in our galaxy alone that they cannot be numbered. We cannot even begin to imagine their brightness and power. The sun itself would blind us if we were to look directly into it for any length of time because its light is so powerful.

Do you know what, beloved? As magnificent and brilliant as the starry hosts are, Jesus did not refer them as the "light of the world, a city set on a hill." He reserved that title just for you! You are the light of His world. Not the sun as brilliant and amazing as it is, nor the starry host as magnificent as they are to view against the blackened sky and not even the moon who governs all those starry hosts. But it is you, beloved, only you. God chose you to light His world…to show His glory like none other. Are you ready to get started beloved? Pray before you begin.

Jesus said in Matthew 5:14, *"You are the light of the world. A city set on a hill cannot be hidden."* Yesterday, we learned that light was never intended to be hidden, just like a lamp that is lit should not be put under a table. Instead that lamp is to be put out so all can see and so that the entire room can be illuminated. Jesus tells us this same truth here in verse 14. What does he compare the light of the world to?

He compares us to a city, doesn't He? It's no ordinary city. He tells us that it is a city that cannot be hidden. What made this city different? Why could it be seen?

Have you ever driven through the mountains at night, beloved? How dark it can be as you wind through the narrow passes that lead you across the mountains. You can travel for miles and miles and see nothing because the darkness is so great. Then all of a sudden you see it. Lights, beautiful lights, illuminating the darkness in the distance. The closer you get, the more you realize that up atop that mountain is not just a light, but many lights. It's a city! A city set up on a mountain lighting up the darkness that enveloped you as your journeyed that long way up. That city cannot be hidden because there it sits high and lofty in the midst of all the darkness. It lets the travelers know that they are almost there…that they are on the right path and that they'll be out of the darkness soon. That precious city lights the way to the top.

Jesus told His listeners that day that they, too, are a city, but no ordinary city. He said that they were a city set up on a hill. A city that is set up on a hill, beloved, is one that is not hidden from view. What do you think Jesus could have meant by these words, beloved? How are you and I to be a city?

Turn to your Word Windows Section in the back of your book and locate the word meaning for **"city"** as used in Matthew 5:14. Record what you found in the space provided for you.

City

THE BLESSED WOMAN

It can be difficult to understand what Jesus meant when He said we were the light of the world…a city set on a hill that cannot be hidden. It's hard to compare ourselves to a city because it's not a living thing, is it? Jesus was likening us to a city set on a hill with a beautiful picture in mind. This is what I want us to see in today's lesson as we close out the week together. If you will grab hold of this picture and see it in its fullest light your life will be forever changed. Does Jesus consider you to be a city? Why? How is that possible? What does that mean to us?

I want us to look at a beautiful passage that gives us wonderful insight into this city that we are to be. It is found in Isaiah 62, which is typed out for you at the end of this week's lesson. Take a few moments to read it through. Once you've finished, go back through and mark every reference to God's people by drawing a box around each with the color of your choosing. It will be every pronoun or noun that refers to the cities, Zion or Jerusalem, land, you, your, or city. Take your time, beloved, for there are a lot of these and I don't want you to miss any of them

What a wonderful city we find in Isaiah 62. According to verse 1, what two things illuminate the city of God?

1. _____

2._____

God tells us that your salvation is a torch that is burning and your righteousness will go forth like brightness. If our salvation is likened to a torch and our righteousness as brightness, then what does that tell us?

_____

_____

In other words, will these things be visible? Can you see a torch in a dark place? Is brightness easily hidden?

_____

There are four things I want us to see about this city of God: her appearance, her sound, her future, and her testimony. We have already marked every reference to this city and there is much to see about her. Isaiah Chapter 62 can easily be divided into these four sections. I have listed these divisions for you. As you go through each one, go back through the text and refer to your markings. There is much to see about this beloved city of God. Take your time, precious student, making sure not to rush this assignment and remembering that Jesus likened you unto a city... this city.

The Appearance of This City (verses 1-5)

According to these verses, how is this city described in appearance?

_____

_____

_____

_____

The Sound Coming from This City (verses 6-7)

According these verses, what is the sound or cry coming from this city? Who are they and what are they saying?

_____

_____

_____

_____

The Future of This City (verses 8-9)

According to these verses, what will the future of this city be like? What promises are given?

_____

_____

_____

_____

The Testimony of This City (verses 10-12)

According to these verses, what is the testimony of this city? What was done for this city and by whom?

_____

_____

_____

_____

This city, beloved, is a picture of you! You are this beloved city…God's delight. You are not just a city, you are His city. In this city, the lights never go out for they are burning with the eternal flames of God's love and grace. This is that city set on a hill; the life that God delights Himself in…the city that God smiles upon. Your light is the radiance of His face as He rejoices over you! Once just a small flame, it now burns all the more brighter. Proverbs 4:18 says, *"But the path of the righteous is like the light of dawn, that shines brighter and brighter until the full day."*

Scientists tell us that our universe, as massive as it is already, is continuously growing. Stars are forming constantly! What is God trying to show us through

His creation… through His word? Light is ever changing. Just as it is ever changing in our universe, it is ever changing within us as well. So we can know that…

Principle
Light is not to remain as it began

Jesus said in John 9:5, *"While I am in the world, I am the light of the world."* According to this verse, if Jesus is in you and you are in the world, then what are you and why?

_____

_____

You are a torch that is burning! The day you received Jesus Christ as your personal Savior, He came to dwell inside of you and the darkness was replaced with the light of Himself. Let me show you this in scripture. Turn to I Peter 2:9. According to this verse, where did Jesus call you out of and what did He call you into?

_____

_____

Your light doesn't stop here. The day you became a child of God…a child of the King, you were at that moment a single light. But Jesus said you are a "city set on a hill." You were not meant to remain alone as a single light, but rather you were saved to be a city of lights. Why? Because light was never intended to remain as it began, but to grow brighter and brighter adding more and more lights until there no longer remains any darkness.

Because light was never created to remain as it began…

Benefit
Others can find their way out of the darkness

Your light was intended to become a city so that others will find their way out of the darkness. Your city must be bright to pierce the great darkness that abounds and it must be set high upon the hills of glory to bring them up out of the miry pit. From one life, a city of lives can be birthed and from one light, a city of lights can come forth and the world will look on with awe and wonder. Where there once was darkness there now is a beloved city found by the Light of the World.

In speaking of the city of God, Revelation 21:23 says…

"And the city has no need of the sun or of the moon to shine on it, for the glory of God has illumined it, and its lamp is the Lamb."

Oh beloved, every city has a story to tell; a story to pass down to the next generation; a glorious story to tell to their children and their children's children so that a generation yet to be created will praise the Lord. Oh beautiful city that you are, precious student, may your lights never go out. May they burn all the more brighter until you behold the face of your sweet savior.

The Lord has shown us many wonderful truths this week as we have opened His word together. Before we review them, take time to read over your memory verse for this week making sure you can say it from memory.

We've looked at the power of salt and light this week. So we won't forget what we've learned, let's review our principles and benefits.

Week in Review

Principle # 1: *Salt must be poured out*
Benefit: *It becomes a powerful force upon the earth*

Principle # 2: *Salt is to remain pure*
Benefit: *It will accomplish the Lord's purpose*

Principle #3: *Light is to be seen*
Benefit: *What is hidden in the darkness will be revealed*

Principle #4: *Light is not to remain as it began*
Benefit: *Others can find their way out of darkness*

As we close our time together, beloved, let's look inward and see what these truths mean to our lives. How have, or how will, they change us?

Personal Evaluation

Are you pure, beloved? Are you useful to the Master's hand?

Are you making a difference in the lives of others?

Does your life point others to the cross of Calvary that they might be saved?

Are you a single light standing alone, or are you a brilliant city set up on a hill?

I know these questions are not easy, beloved. Before these truths ever reach you, God has already grabbed me with them! It's so important that we realize that we are salt…we are light. It's not something we strive toward. It is a fact. It is a fact that Jesus spoke very plainly about. He wanted you and me to understand what we are, because what we are, beloved, will affect what we do.

It's been a powerful week, hasn't it? As we close out our week together, why don't you just take the time to thank Jesus for saving you? Tell Him how much you love Him. Ask Him to make you pure salt. Ask Him to change your life so powerfully that your life is that city set on a hill that is so bright that the darkness flees.

I love and appreciate you so very much, precious daughter of the King. I pray I will see you in our teaching session together.

Isaiah 62

¹*For Zion's sake I will not keep silent, and for Jerusalem's sake I will not keep quiet, until her righteousness goes forth like brightness, and her salvation like a torch that is burning.*

²*The nations will see your righteousness, and all kings your glory; and you will be called by a new name which the mouth of the Lord will designate.*

³*You will be a crown of beauty in the hand of the Lord, and a royal diadem in the hand of your God.*

⁴*It will no longer be said of you, "Forsaken", nor to your land will it any longer be said, "Desolate"; but you will be called, "My delight is in her," and your land, "Married"; for the Lord delights in you, and to Him your land will be married.*

⁵*For as a young man marries a virgin, so your sons will marry you; as the bridegroom rejoices over the bride, so your God will rejoice over you.*

⁶*On your walls, O Jerusalem, I have appointed watchmen; all day and night they will never keep silent.*

⁷*You who remind the Lord, take no rest for yourselves; and give Him no rest until He establishes and makes Jerusalem a praise in the earth.*

⁸*The Lord has sworn by His right hand and by His strong arm, "I will never again give your grain as food for your enemies; nor will foreigners drink your new wine for which you have labored."*

⁹*But those garner it will eat it and praise the Lord; and those who gather it will drink it in the courts of My sanctuary.*

¹⁰*Go through, go through the gates, clear the way for the people; build up, build up the highway, remove the stones, lift up a standard over the peoples.*

¹¹*Behold, the Lord has proclaimed to the end of the earth, say to the daughter of Zion, "Lo, your salvation comes; behold His reward is with Him, and His recompense before Him."*

¹²*And they will call them, "The holy people, the redeemed of the Lord"; and you will be called, "Sought out, a city not forsaken."*

LESSON EIGHT
Kingdom Living

Day One

Well beloved, we have reached our final week together in their journey that has taken us to the Sermon on the Mount. What a journey it has been so far as we have sat at the feet of Jesus and listened to His words. We have plummeted the poverty of the poor in spirit. We have wept with those who mourn, suffered with those who are persecuted for their faith, hungered and thirsted for righteousness, extended mercy, and walked in the shoes of the blessed peacemaker. We have seen the reflection of God as we peered with unveiled eyes into the heart of the pure. We have traveled to the hills of the beautiful city of God and have poured out the salt of the earth that it may accomplish God's purpose. Again, beloved, what a journey it has been thus far!

But these steps are only the beginning of what should be a life long journey…a life journey lived up on the mount of Jesus Himself, unveiling the blessed life before the eyes of the world. But where do we begin, beloved? How are we to live the blessed life every day of our lives, moment by moment? This blessed life is what Jesus intends for us to have. But how? This will be our goal as we open God's Word this week. Pray before you begin, asking God to speak to your heart in a personal way. Ask Him to teach you His ways that you may know Him.

THE BLESSED WOMAN

Let's begin this week's study by reading through our main text of study found in Matthew Chapters 5, 6 and 7. These chapters should be a part of you by now precious student, because we have continued to read through them over and over. Though we cannot cover all three of these chapters in depth, I think it's vital that you gain a full understanding of what's covered in the entire Sermon on the Mount. Our last week together will be spent drawing out the principles in the teachings that follow the "blesseds" or the "beatitudes" that Jesus spoke of.

Read through Matthew 5:17-48, which, as you know, is typed out in the back of your study book. As you read through these verses, I want you to take note of two phrases that Jesus uses over and over again. He says: *"You have heard"* and *"I say to you"* many times in just these few verses alone. As you read through Matthew 5:17-48, I want you to highlight these two phrases so they will stand out from one another. Mark them with the following colors.

"You have heard" (mark in yellow)
"I say to you" (mark in red)

Once you've finished your markings, make a list of the issues that Jesus covered in these verses. List the subjects that were covered to help give us an overview of what Jesus was speaking of.

_____

_____

_____

_____

_____

What do you think Jesus is trying to tell His listeners by using these two phrases?

_____

_____

Jesus wanted His audience to know that it is not important what others have said, or what you have heard in the past. What you should know and listen to are the words of the Lord. It's important to know what God says, not man. You see, beloved, the people in Jesus' day had come to the place where they held the word of man as the law of their lives. They had embraced the wisdom of man even when it did not line up with the will of God. To embrace one is to reject the other.

Jesus had just given eight *"blesseds"* to these precious listeners. Now, He was going to tell them how to live accordingly. The blessed life, according to His teaching, according to what He has said, will live by the guidelines and principles that have been given by the Father. It does not matter what others have taught about the blessed life. It only matters what Jesus tells us. This is a pattern that we cannot miss, beloved. The pattern that Jesus lays out in Matthew 5, 6 and 7 is the lifestyle of those who are part of the Kingdom of God. It's Kingdom Living, beloved.

To help us understand and see this pattern for Kingdom Living, let's look back at Matthew 5:17-18. These verses cover four basic areas of our lives and are as follows:

I. *Our Relationships* (vs. 17-26)

II. *Our Weaknesses* (vs. 27-32)

III. *Our Commitments* (vs. 33-37)

IV. *Our Love* (vs. 38-48)

Let's look at each of these individually and how they affect our lives. This will not be an in depth look because of time, beloved, but we will cover these a little more in depth in the teaching session.

Our Relationships

Jesus speaks about our relationships out in the world and with one another in verses 17-27. He covers the whole gamut of relationships from emotions, communications, forgiveness, and just the basics of how to get along with one another. According to these verses, how important is it that we are right with one another?

_____

_____

Jesus said that being at peace with one another is so important that you are not even to make an offering to the Lord if there is someone you are not right with. It's better to leave your service momentarily and make it right, than to continue when there is discord. So what is Jesus telling us by this? Your relationships affect your service to the Lord.

According to verses 21 and 22, are the emotions that we feel toward one another important? What does he compare sinful emotions to?

_____

_____

It's pretty convicting to know that our emotions can be just as sinful as the act of committing murder or some other sin against another person. God looks at our heart, beloved, for the heart is the dwelling place of not only our emotions, but also the Lord if we are His disciples. In verse 22, Jesus also speaks about the words we use with one another. Based on this verse, do you think there are consequences for the words we use with one another?

_____

_____

Look up James 1:26. According to this verse, what do we learn about the importance of our words?

_____

_____

Concerning our words, Jesus goes on to say in Matthew 12:36-37: *"But I tell you that every careless word that people speak they shall give an accounting for it in the day of judgment. For by your words you will be justified, and by your words you will be condemned."* Kingdom Living will exercise wisdom by choosing words that edify or build up; words of grace seasoned as with salt (*Colossians 4:6*). They will be slow to speak and quick to hear (*James 1:19*). Jesus wanted us to know that words are powerful. They can be used for good and evil. Words affect our relationships and Kingdom Living will recognize the power of the tongue.

Our Weakness

Most people would not be comfortable admitting their weaknesses. Jesus recognized that we will have areas of weaknesses in our lives, but it's how we respond to these weaknesses that is important. According to verses 27-28, can we have a weakness of the eyes? Is it just what we look at, or is it how we look at things, as well?

_____

_____

How are we to handle the lust of the eyes according to Jesus in verse 29?

_____

_____

Beloved, let me clarify something in this verse. Jesus is not saying for us to go home and pluck out our eyes because we are lusting with them. What I believe He is saying here is that whatever our weaknesses are, we are not to allow ourselves to be put in a position that will allow weaknesses to rule over us. Why? Because Jesus tells us in Matthew 26:31, the spirit is willing, but the flesh is weak. In this same verse He tells His disciples to keep watching and praying so they would not enter into temptation. He knew of their weaknesses and He knows of ours, beloved. Look up the following verses and record what you learned about the flesh and how to deal with it.

• **Galatians 5:13-21**

_____

_____

_____

• **Galatians 6:8**

_____

_____

_____

So what does this mean to you and me regarding our areas of weaknesses? Don't give them opportunities to win. Feed your spirit and starve your flesh.

Our Commitments

Jesus covers a subject that is touchy in today's world: commitments. Commitments are almost considered outdated in some areas of life such as marriage, parenting, jobs, taxes, bills, and even areas of service in the church or community. Gone are the days when people gave you their word they would do something you never wondered if they would. Today in America, 1 in every

3 marriages will end in divorce because there is no commitment. Everyday children are abandoned by their parents and the unemployment rate continues to soar because people simply have no commitment to their jobs or to their families. Churches around the world are hurting for workers for different areas of ministry because they can't find people who are committed to serving the Lord. The Lord said that the fields are white unto Harvest but there are few workers. Why, beloved? Because commitment is lacking.

According to verse 37, what should our answers be? What do you think Jesus meant by this?

_____

_____

Jesus wasn't just telling us to have a simple answer. He was wanting us to understand when we say 'yes', our 'yes' should mean 'yes.' In other words…our "I do's" should mean just that…"I do." We should be people of integrity…people who honor their word. If you say no to something, beloved, then stand firm and don't vacillate. To simplify this truth: mean what you say.

How would living by this truth affect the way you deal with your children?

_____

_____

How awesome that would be for us parents if we would let our 'yes' mean 'yes,' and our 'no' mean 'no.' Have you ever allowed your children to talk your 'no' into a 'yes?' I have and usually regretted it. Jesus was speaking of a determination to stand firm on your convictions and to honor your word. What powerful words to apply to every area in our lives. Can you imagine how it would affect your business, your home, your job, your relationships, or your ministry? Your life would have a tremendous affect on the lives of countless others.

Our Love

Love is a word that is used so lightly today and abused too often; an emotion that can fade away almost as quickly as it arrived. It is deemed just a feeling and is conditional at best because emotions are unstable at times and misleading. Love is misunderstood and many times used as a form of manipulation in our society because people want to be loved so desperately. Most people in their lifetime will never experience true, never ending, and unconditional love. God is love and we were created in His image. We were created by God to love and to be loved with the love that can only come from Him. Because this is true, we will never be fully satisfied with any other kind of love.

Jesus said that love is so important that out of all the commandments of God, it is the greatest. Furthermore, it is by love the whole world will know that we belong to Him. This is a sign to the world; a mark, that we are followers of Jesus Christ. Love is the most powerful force on earth; so powerful, that it moved the heart of God to send His only Son to die for your sins.

In verses 38-46, Jesus tells us who we are to love, and how we are to love. What does He tell us concerning love?

_____

_____

_____

Turn to your Word Windows Section and look up the definition for the word **"love"** as used in these verses. Record your findings in the space provided for you.

Love

_____

_____

Is our love to have conditions or to be selective? Is there a limit to this kind of love? Are we to love our enemies the same way we love those who are not our enemies?

_____

_____

Look up the following verses and record what you learn about love from each.

- **I John 3:16-23**

_____

_____

_____

- **I John 4:9-21**

_____

_____

_____

- **I Corinthians 13:1-13**

_____

_____

_____

- **Ephesians 5:1**

_____

_____

_____

In verse 48, Jesus said that we were to be perfect as God is perfect. I think you probably feel as I do regarding this: "I will never be perfect," or "How can I be perfect?" Is this an unreasonable command for us, beloved? To help us understand this commandment a little better, turn to your Word Windows Section and find the definition for the word **"perfect."** Write out your findings in the space provided for you.

Perfect

_____

_____

Based on the definition of the word, **"perfect"**, what do you think Jesus meant when He said we are to be perfect as God is perfect?

_____

_____

The key to being perfect, beloved, is found in its meaning. When Jesus said that we were to be perfect as God is perfect He was telling us that we have everything we need from God to be all that God wants us to be. We are complete in Him.

It will be evident in our relationships, our jobs, our families, our attitudes, our churches, our service and ministry. There is no area of our lives that Kingdom Living should not dominate and should not be evident. We often times try to pick and choose where we want to apply God's truths or implement God's principles into our decisions, our relationships etc. For example, we may be faithful in attending church and in serving the Lord, but be harboring unforgiveness. We may love our neighbor as our self, but not tithe as we should. We might be giving all we have to the poor, yet slandering our fellow church members. Someone might be the hardest working servant in their church, but have no prayer life. The list could go on and on.

Kingdom Living is not just a Sunday affair. You cannot separate the follower of Christ from Kingdom Living. They are one in the same. This brings us to our first principle on Kingdom Living.

Principle
Kingdom living affects every aspect of our lives

Typed out for you is Matthew 7:21. Take a minute to read over it and answer the question that follows.

Matthew 7:21

"Not everyone who says to Me, 'Lord, Lord,' will enter the Kingdom of Heaven, but he who does the will of My Father who is in heaven will enter."

According to this verse, who is the one that will enter the Kingdom of Heaven?

You see, beloved, those who will enter the Kingdom of God will have a certain lifestyle, certain characteristics. This lifestyle involves doing the will of God. This is what Kingdom Living is, living according to the will of God. In other words, they live to please God and honor God in all they say, and in all they are. They desire to be what God wants them to be. Remember, God's Will is about being rather than doing. Do you remember why, beloved? Because what you are will determine what you do.

Galatians 2:20 says…

"I have been crucified with Christ; and it is no longer I who live, but Christ lives in me; and the life which I now live in the flesh I live by faith in the Son of God, who loved me and gave Himself up for me."

When we embrace Kingdom Living something amazing happens…

Benefit
We live for a higher purpose

We find that we are living for something much greater than ourselves! We understand that we have a purpose for living and it's not us! Amen? Jesus told His disciples that whoever would lose their life for His sake would find it. The saddest life of all, precious student, is the one that is lived for itself. As we close our day of study together, take a few moments and read over your memory verse for this week.

Memory Verse

Matthew 6:19-20

"Do not store up for yourselves treasures on earth, where moth and rust destroy, and where thieves break in and steal. But store up for yourselves treasures in heaven, where neither moth nor rust destroys, and where thieves do not break in or steal."

How I appreciate you, precious student. This has been a lengthy lesson today and I pray that you will stay the course because we are almost finished.

What a blessing you are to the heart of your Heavenly Father. He is looking down and smiling upon you, beloved, because He loves for us to love His Word.

I will look for you on Day Two! Hang in there.

Day Two

The principles of Kingdom Living should govern every area of our lives. There is no area, no behavior, no decision, no emotion, no job, no ministry, no relationship, no ideology, and no character that it does not have the right to govern. Kingdom Living is about living for the Kingdom of God and not yourself, for others or for any other reason or thing. Find those whose life is set on Kingdom Living and you will find the "blessed" life.

Don't let the world, a church, a preacher or teacher, bottle their ideology of what a blessed life is and sell it to you, precious student. Contrary to popular belief, the blessed life is not "health and prosperity." If this were true, then Jesus would have mentioned this at some point during His sermon on what the "blessed" life is. Blessedness is not a possession but rather it is a position. Jesus spoke of many things to His listeners that day so long ago. So many in fact that we could never begin to touch the hem of them in one study. After Jesus gave the eight "blesseds," He followed them by laying out for us the principles of Kingdom Living. From yesterday's study, we learned that Kingdom Living affects every area giving us a higher purpose for living; that higher purpose being the Kingdom of God. As always, take time to stop and pray before you begin seeking God's blessings upon your study time. He is the source of all wisdom and the One who reveals truth.

Turn to Matthew 6 and 7 located in the back of your study book and read through them once to refresh your memory. Now go back and read through them a second time but this time as you do, I want you to mark every reference to the word "hypocrite" (or hypocrites) by drawing a circle around it with the color pencil of your choice. Remember to include all pronouns referring to this word as well.

What did you learn about hypocrites from marking the text? Make a list in the space provided.

The Hypocrite

_____

_____

_____

_____

_____

_____

Turn to your Word Windows Section and look up the definition for the word **"hypocrite"** as used here in Matthew 6 and 7. Record your findings in the space provided.

Hypocrite

_____

_____

_____

Hypocrisy in its simplest form means: to wear a mask. Jesus spoke of several areas where we are not to wear a mask.

Based on your markings, what areas of our lives did Jesus address concerning hypocrisy?

_____

_____

To make sure we don't miss any of these areas, see if you can fill in the blanks of the sentences below concerning hypocrisy. I have mentioned the verse that applies for each to help you find the answer.

• According to Matthew 6:1 we are not to be a hypocrite by practicing our_____ before others to be noticed by them.

• Matthew 6:2-4 tells us not to be hypocritical in our _____ in order to be honored by others.

• Based on Matthew 6:5 we are not be a hypocrite when we _____so others will see us.

• Matthew 6:16 tells us not to be a hypocrite when we _____ by putting on a gloomy face so others will know what we've been doing.

• Matthew 7:5 teaches that we are not to be a hypocrite in _____our brothers and sisters when we have greater sin in our own lives.

Every time we practice our righteousness before men just so they will be impressed with us or so they will pick us for a position in our church, or job, etc, then we are being deceitful. Every time we give so people in the church will respect us, then we are being deceitful. Every time we pray or fast in such a way that others will notice, then we are deceiving others. If we sit in condemnation of our sisters when we are so sinful ourselves, then we are wearing the mask of hypocrisy. When we pretend to be someone's friend to their face and act differently behind their back, then we are being deceitful. Why? Because wearing a mask is deceit.

Think about it, beloved, what is a mask for? Why would someone wear one?

_____

_____

A mask is worn to cover up ones true identity. We wear many different masks in our lives, beloved. Sometimes we wear them with our husbands, our children, at our workplace, when the preacher comes to visit, singing in the choir, teaching a Sunday school class, in front of our neighbors or friends. We all have them and we've all worn them at one time or another.

Look up the following verses that deal with hypocrisy and note what you learn beside each.

- **I Peter 2:1**

_____

_____

_____

- **Matthew 23: 23-28**

_____

_____

_____

- **I Timothy 4:1-3**

_____

_____

_____

- **James 3:17**

_____

_____

_____

Based on some of the verses you've looked at, how would you describe hypocrisy as God views it?

_____

_____

What fruit comes from hypocrisy? What is its end result in the lives of people?

_____

_____

In the Old Testament, the Hebrew word for "hypocrite" is used to mean or describe the godless man, the man with no morals, no future, and no hope. The word "hypocrite" has strong meaning, beloved, and it is never used favorably in the Word of God. At the base of every act of hypocrisy you will find wrong motives. Every act of the hypocrite is conducted on the basis of ungodly motives. Desiring to be recognized by others is ungodly. Desiring the applause and respect of people or organizations is ungodly. Choosing to act a certain way or do a particular thing just so others will be impressed with you is ungodly. All of these things have no room in Kingdom Living. Jesus makes it clear in Matthew 6 and 7 that…

Principle
Kingdom living wears no mask

There is no place and no room for hypocrisy in Kingdom Living because pure motives are necessary when we are living for the Kingdom of God. Remember the blessedness, "blessed are the pure in heart?" The pure in heart will have pure motives.

Why do we so easily put on a mask? Wouldn't it be easier to be ourselves? Do you know why we don't want to remove our masks, beloved? It's not so much that don't want others to see what's there. I believe it's because we don't want to see or be reminded of what's there. The truth is hard to face, beloved, especially when it's our face. Typed out for you is James 1:22-24. Read through it and answer the questions that follow.

James 1:22-25

"But prove yourselves doers of the word, and not merely hearers who delude themselves. For if anyone is a hearer of the word and not a doer, he is like a man who looks at his natural face in a mirror; for once he has looked at himself and gone away, he has immediately forgotten what kind of person he was. But one who looks intently at the perfect law, the law of liberty, and abides by it, not having become a forgetful hearer but an effectual doer, this man will be blessed in what he does."

Based on these verses, the person who is not a doer of the Word of God will be like what kind of person?

_____

_____

What kind of face is mentioned in this verse?

_____

To help us better understand what is meant by the term "**natural**" turn to your Word Windows Section in the back and locate the meaning. Write what you discover in the space provided.

Natural

_____

_____

Did you notice the word "Genesis" (genesis in the Greek) in there, beloved? What do you think this could mean? You see, beloved, when we look at our natural face, we are looking at ourselves as we truly are. It's a looking at self, not as others see you, or how you see yourselves compared to others, but rather it's looking at you as God looks at you. Nothing is hidden from God. It's to see our self with the mask off! You cannot see who you are, beloved, when you are wearing a mask. Just as the man who looks in the mirror and walks away, you, too, will forget what you look like when you walk away from who you really are by putting on a mask.

Because Kingdom Living wears no mask, then the following is true…

Benefit
Hypocrisy will vanish

You may be revealed, beloved, but hypocrisy will vanish. How will you correct what needs to be made right in your life if you never stop and take the time to look at what's there? Why don't you stop right now and ask God to show you the masks that are in your life. Start by allowing God to remove them, beloved. There's no need to worry about what God will think because He already knows what's behind the masks we wear. And you know what, precious student? He loves the person that is behind the mask. When Jesus went to the cross he saw your face, not a mask. It was your face that He loved so much that He chose to die. Do you know what else, beloved? He smiles when He thinks of what that person will become once they remove their masks. God doesn't want the pretender, He wants you.

Hypocrisy is always difficult to deal with because we become so comfortable wearing our mask. There are many reasons why we put on the mask, from fear of rejection to pride. You see, we can be whatever we want to be temporarily and not have to deal with the real us. We can put that off for a later date of our choosing. But no matter how long we wear it, the mask will never change the face that lies beneath. The mask may change, but the face never will; the face that will someday look intently into the very face of God, for there will be no masks in heaven. And so it is with Kingdom Living as well.

I want to leave you with these thoughts…

What masks are you wearing, beloved? What would it take for you to remove them? Why do you wear the masks you are wearing? Who are you trying to please or impress with your masks? Find the reason why you put on your masks and there you will also find your reason for living.

Thank you for studying so diligently with me today. Take a few moments and review your memory verse for this week. See you on Day Three.

Day Three

As we are discovering, Kingdom Living requires full surrender and total honesty. Kingdom Living is not for those who are looking for the easy road nor is it for the faint hearted. It is not for the lazy or the one who wants to chart his own course in life. Most certainly it is not for the person who believes they can choose their own morals, write their own standards or have the right to choose to do what makes them happy. The younger generation is considered to be the "exploration generation" because they are exploring many things including their sexuality, their religious beliefs, their future, and much more. They base this need for "exploration" on the need to find out who they are individually. It's a "find what makes you happy" generation that is coming up before our very eyes which will affect the future government. A past president once said: *"The beliefs of one generation will be the law of the government in the next."*

This is why it is vital, beloved, that we learn Kingdom Living in order to model it to our children and our children's children. Kingdom Living has to be real in the eyes of unbelievers before they will ever embrace it. It is a dying lifestyle! Where are the true children who belong to the Kingdom of God? I believe that Jesus addressed one of the greatest hindrances to Kingdom Living in Matthew 6:5-13. This will be our course of study today. Pray before you begin, precious student.

Today we are going to look at the power of prayer, how we are to pray, and why we are to pray. Jesus addressed prayer in His Sermon on the Mount and it can and will change our prayer life if we will choose to follow His teachings. Let's begin our study together by reading through Matthew chapter six. We already know that we are to pray with pure motives. We are not to pray in order to impress others with our praying skills or to show how "righteous" we think we are.

Jesus said in verse 9 of this chapter to: *"Pray, then in this way."* Because He used these words, what should that tell us about praying?

_____

_____

Turn to your Word Windows Section and find the definition for the word **"prayer"** as used by Jesus in this verse. Record your findings in the space provided.

Prayer

_____

_____

Prayer is not stationary, beloved. In other words, it is a moving force with God. We tend to see prayer as conversing with God, but it's much more than that. In light of this word meaning, what do you think Jesus was telling us when He said, *"Pray then in this way?"*

_____

_____

I don't believe that Jesus was telling His listeners that when they pray they are only to use this exact wording every time. I do, however, believe that Jesus was giving us a pattern for prayer. Based on the word meaning, I believe He was showing us that prayer is what moves God and it is what should move us as well. Prayer is coming along side of God to do His bidding. Prayer is not just communing with God, it is coming along side Him to accomplish His will upon the earth. Prayer is what builds the Kingdom of God, beloved! I want us to look at the Lord's Prayer and the pattern given to us for praying but first, I want us to look at some verses that deal with prayer.

Look up the following verses and note what you learn about prayer beside each. Note what prayer is for and the effects of prayer. Why are we told to pray? To whom are we to pray? How are we to pray?

- **Matthew 26:41**

_____

_____

_____

- **Matthew 9:37-38**

_____

_____

_____

- **James 5:13-18**

_____

_____

_____

- **II Corinthians 13:7**

_____

_____

_____

- **I Thessalonians 5:17**

_____

_____

_____

- **Philippians 4:6**

_____

_____

_____

Read Jeremiah 31:8-9 that is typed out for you. These verses are speaking of a future day when God was going to gather the nation of Israel and bring them back together in their beloved promised land.

Jeremiah 31:8-9

"Behold I am bringing them from the north country, and I will gather them from the remote parts of the earth, among them the blind and the lame, the woman with child and she who is in labor with child, together; a great company, they will return here.

"With weeping they will come, and by supplication I will lead them; I will make them walk by streams of waters, on a straight path in which they will not stumble; for I am a father to Israel, and Ephraim is My firstborn."

THE BLESSED WOMAN

According to verse nine how was God going to lead them?

_____

_____

God was going to lead them home through supplication; through prayer! Prayer is vital to God's people for Kingdom Living. If we don't pray, beloved, how will we know the way to go? How will God lead us if we are not communing with Him and listening to His voice? This is how we end up in places in our lives that God never intended for us to be. Prayer keeps you on track with your Heavenly Father. We do not have time to do an in depth study of the Lord's Prayer but there are a few things I want us to take note of.

Note the pattern of the prayer that Jesus gave to us in Matthew 6:9-13:

⁹"Our Father Who is in heaven, hallowed be Your name.
¹⁰"Your Kingdom come. Your will be done, on earth as it is in heaven.
¹¹"Give us this day our daily bread.
¹²"And forgive us our debts, as we also have forgiven our debtors.
¹³"And do not lead us into temptation, but deliver us from evil. For Yours is the kingdom and the power and the glory forever. Amen."

Our Approach (vs. 9)

According to verse nine, how are you to approach God when you pray? What is He called?

_____

_____

In our praying we are to come to God as His children because we are. So as His children we can come to Him because He loves His children. We are to praise and revere His name. His wonderful name is to be recognized because His name represents who He is. Turn to your Word Windows Section and find the definition for "**hallowed**" and record what you find in the space provided.

Hallowed

_____

_____

When we pray, beloved, we are to approach God as our Father but we are also to recognize His holiness. Just because He is our Father doesn't mean that we can approach him in a disrespectful way or in a way that does not recognize His holiness. Our approach to God should always be with a reverent heart, knowing that He is a Holy God, but without fear, knowing that He loves us because He is our Father.

Our Desire (vs. 10)

In verse 10 of the Lord's Prayer what is to be the desire of our heart above every other thing?

_____

_____

Because this is the first thing that is prayed for it signifies absolute importance and utter priority. We are to pray for God's Kingdom to come, for it to be made complete. Remember the verses on prayer? We are to ask God to send out laborers unto the fields so His Kingdom can come. We are to pray for His will to be done first and foremost above every other. This is the very heart of Kingdom Living! Kingdom Living is all about what God desires not what we desire. He is the center of Kingdom Living. Everything revolves around Him. Amen?

Our Dependency (vs. 11)

Verse 11 tells us how we are to ask for our needs. What did you notice about praying for our "daily bread?" Did you notice anything significant?

_____

_____

Praying according to Jesus means looking to God for our needs to be met. It's depending on Him "daily," hence the words…"daily bread." We are to look every day to God as a little child looks to his earthly father. This is why we are not told to ask once for God to meet "all" our needs and be done with it. God wants us totally dependent upon Him for everything everyday of our lives. We will forget that we need God if it were any other way, beloved. You will not ask God to meet your daily needs unless you believe He can and that He will. The self-sufficient heart will never depend on God for anything.

Our Attitude (vs.12)

In verse 12, what is the attitude we are to have toward forgiveness?

_____

_____

Do you realize how powerful this line is, beloved? To actually pray that God would forgive you of your sins according to how you forgive others of their sins against you? How many of us could say that this is our attitude toward forgiveness? Jesus wanted His listeners to know that forgiveness is absolutely vital in Kingdom Living. You must forgive just as you have been forgiven. Forgiveness is so important to the heart of God that He sent Jesus so we could have it. When we pray, beloved, there should be no unforgiveness in our heart toward anyone. Do you have a heart that does not hesitate to forgive? Would you hesitate to forgive someone if your forgiveness from God was based on whether or not you forgave? In other words…"let my forgiveness be based upon how I forgive others." Pretty powerful isn't it, beloved?

The Lord's Prayer is not a prayer to be recited when we don't know what to pray. It is not to be taken lightly. Its words are powerful.

Our Determination (vs. 13)

According to verse 13, what should we be determined not to do? What are we to ask of God?

_____

_____

This should be the greatest fear of every Christian: that we would enter into temptation and sin against God. We should be afraid of sin in our lives; so afraid that we flee at the first sign of temptation; so afraid that we pray daily that God would keep us from the path that would lead to temptation because it would lead to sin. Beloved, to pray these words is to recognize our weaknesses. It's when we think we are beyond stumbling that we will fall.

Wise is the woman who recognizes that she is weak and learns to totally depend on God for everything; the woman who cannot make it one day, one moment without prayer because it is her lifeline to the Father…her Father. This is the woman who will lift her eyes heavenward and raise her voice to say: "Yours is the kingdom and the power and the glory forever. Amen," because she has believed Her Father to be everything she needs and in believing, found Him to be everything she wants.

This woman knows….

Principle
Praying is the lifeline of Kingdom Living

Just as blood is the lifeline for the body, prayer is the lifeline for Kingdom Living. You cannot make it without it. You will not further the Kingdom of God apart from it. You will fail utterly without it. God works through prayer!

When prayer is the lifeline of Kingdom Living then…

Benefit
The Kingdom of God is built

Do you remember the words of Jesus in Matthew 6:10? The first thing we are to pray for beloved is: *"Thy Kingdom come!"* Our hearts' cry should be for the Kingdom of God to come, or to be built, and that will not happen apart from the lifeline of prayer.

Oh precious daughter of the Living God, what a wonderful plan He has for your life! It is a plan written just for you by His sovereign hand. He desires to have all of you, every thought, every desire, every plan, in every area. Kingdom Living is not for the weak or fainthearted and it is not for the prayerless woman. We must be women of prayer if we are going to be about Kingdom Living. I have heard it said that we are not to pray for the work of God because prayer is the work of God. This puts a new perspective on things doesn't it, beloved? Everything depends on prayer! Prayer to God that is!

May I leave you some personal questions to ponder, my friend? What is your prayer life like? Do you have a prayer life? Do you believe that prayer is your life, beloved? Do you recognize the need to pray at all times and not just in times of trouble? More importantly, what are you going to do to improve your prayer life? What would God want you to do?

You have worked so very hard today, beloved, and I am so proud of you. Take a few moments and review your memory verse for this week. One more day to go!

Day Four

Well, beloved, it's our final day together. We may be ending this work but it is God who is beginning a new work; a new work in your life that will bring Him greater glory and greater pleasure. Have you ever wondered, "Lord, what is your purpose for my life?" If you are like me, then you've asked that question many times throughout your life. Although we may be constantly changing, His purpose for us never does. His plans were formed long ago and He is working them out with perfect faithfulness. Although I cannot tell you what His specific plan is for your life, I can tell you what His purpose is for you. I can tell you this, beloved, because He told us Himself in His Sermon on the Mount. Are you ready to journey there again today and see what that purpose is? Pray before you begin, beloved, and we'll get started.

Let's begin our study time together by reading through Matthew Chapters 5, 6 and 7. As you know, we have soaked in these chapters by reading them through over and over again. By now the words of Jesus should be branded upon your memory forever. Truth can never be taken from you, beloved, and it will never mislead you.

Once you've finished reading through these chapters, I want you to go back to Chapter Six and read through it once more. As you do this, mark every reference to the word "worry" by underlining it with the colored pencil of your choice. Based on your markings, what did you note about "worry" from this passage? What things are listed that we worry about?

Worry

_____

_____

_____

_____

Five times Jesus uses the word "worry." Do you think He's trying to make a point about worrying? Absolutely. To give us better insight into Jesus' teaching, turn to your Word Windows Section and find the definition for the word "**worry**." The King James Version translates the word "worry" with the phrase: "take no thought." Record your findings in the space provided.

Worry *(take no thought)*

_____

_____

Worry is a thief that robs us of so many things including our peace, our joy and our confidence. It steals our sleep in the night and threatens our relationships in the day. It destroys the brightness of the future and the potential of the present. Jesus understood what it was like to face the battle of worry. He knows what it is like to live upon this earth and face the problems of life. Jesus told His listeners not to worry about their needs, the number of days of their life, or even the things of the future that might come into their lives. We are not to concern ourselves with these things. In fact, Jesus taught his listeners the secret to having all of their needs met! He taught them the secret of the blessed life because the blessed life is living a life without worry…without fear! Let's look at this secret.

Typed out for you is Matthew 6:33.

Matthew 6:33

"But seek first His kingdom and His righteousness, and all these things will be added to you."

What two things are we to seek?

1._____

2._____

What do you think it means to seek something? What would that involve?

_____

_____

Let's make sure we understand what it means to seek after something according to God. Turn to your Word Windows Section and locate the definition for the word "**seek**" as used in Matthew 6:33. Record your findings in the space provided.

Seek

_____

_____

_____

In light of this word meaning, look up the following verses and list what you learned from each. Note where our focus, and our attention is to be. What are we to seek? What are we not to seek? Where should our focus not be?

- **Colossians 3:1-2**

_____

_____

_____

- **Matthew 16:23-25**

_____

_____

_____

- **Philippians 3:17-21**

_____

_____

_____

The question remains, precious student: What are you seeking? Our affections should not be set on anything found on this earth. They should be directed heavenward to the place where eternity will be spent. It's living with eternity before your eyes each and every day. This is a conscious choice, beloved, that is made over and over again. There are many who seek their own kingdoms and not the Kingdom of God. They are building their kingdoms upon the earth where moth and rust destroy. Jesus isn't looking for Kingdom Builders, He is looking for Kingdom Seekers. Before the Kingdom of God can ever be built it must be first sought after. It's in the seeking that God will bless and build His kingdom. It's important that we understand that our role is not the role of a builder but the role of a seeker. Note what Jesus said to Peter concerning His church or His Kingdom.

Matthew 16:15-18

"He said to them, 'But who do you say that I am?' Simon Peter answered, 'You are the Christ, the Son of the living God.' And Jesus said to him, 'Blessed are you, Simon Barjona, because flesh and blood did not reveal this to you, but My Father who is in Heaven. I also say to you that you are Peter, and upon this rock I will build My Church (or Kingdom); and the gates of Hades will not overpower it.'"

Who is going to build the Lord's church or the Lord's Kingdom?

_____

Why do you think this might be significant, beloved? Why are we not called the builders?

_____

_____

Look up the following verses and note what you learned from each.

•**Psalm 127:1**

_____

_____

_____

• **Hebrews 11:8-10**

_____

_____

_____

God never intended for us to be the builders, beloved! He did, however, intend for us to be seekers of His Kingdom. God will use the lives of those who seek His Kingdom to build His Kingdom. Are you seeking, beloved, or are you trying to build something God never intended for you to do? This is why we tire in our flesh many times when serving in the Church or working in Ministry. We are trying to be the Master builders instead of the Master seekers! We are to be seekers of His Kingdom, but He didn't stop here. Jesus didn't say we were to just seek first His Kingdom. But He also told us we were to seek His righteousness as well.

Beloved, why do you think Jesus doesn't tell us to only seek His Kingdom? Wouldn't that have been enough? Didn't He tell us not to seek righteousness itself but to seek His righteousness? What do you think this means? Why is it important to seek both?

_____

_____

_____

At the beginning of this study we looked at the word meaning for **"righteousness"** as used in Jesus' Sermon on the Mount. Take a minute and turn to your Word Windows Section and review the meaning of this word.

Turn to Isaiah 64:6. According to this verse, what is our righteousness compared to?

_____

There are many who not only build their own Kingdoms, but they write the laws of their own righteousness. It's not our righteousness that is needed or demanded by God. Rather it is important to understand that it is His righteousness that we are to seek. The very best that we could ever muster in our own strength, no matter how good we are, would be as filthy rags in the eyes of God. We live in a generation that believes each person must decide what is right or wrong; that each person must decide what is truth and what is not. God gave us a free will, beloved, but never did He give to us the authority to write the standard or change the standards of His Word...His righteousness. That is reserved for Him and Him alone. There are absolutes, precious student, and they are the very Words of God.

We must seek God's Kingdom and His righteousness at the same time. If we don't, we would have no standard of measure. This is why it is so important to have the two together. This is how we will know if we are building God's Kingdom or man's kingdom. It's a sign to us, beloved.

Turn to Matthew 7: 15-23 and note what you learn about the Lord's work verses man's work.

_____

_____

_____

Jesus gave us fair warning that there would be those who seek to build their own kingdoms. They may perform great miracles, even prophesying and casting out demons in the name of Jesus. How marvelous this sounds, doesn't it, precious student? Yet Jesus said to these miracle workers that He did not know them. According to these same verses, how will we know those who are of God and about His Kingdom?

_____

_____

Jesus describes this same truth further in reference to the Kingdom of God in Matthew Chapter 13:24-30. Read these verses and note what is said about the false brethren. Note where they are and why they remain where they are. What will happen to them in the end? How did they get where they were?

_____

_____

_____

At what point did the tares become evident?

_____

_____

We may not know that they are there, beloved, until growth is happening. We must know that among the followers of Christ are also the false teachers. Those who would seek to choke out the work of God to accomplish their own work because they want to receive the praise of man. Jesus wanted us to be able to recognize these false teachers, these false brethren. He told us in the Sermon on the Mount that we will know them by their fruit. Do you see it, beloved? It was only when the wheat was sprouting and bearing grain that the tares were evident. Why? If the wheat doesn't bear forth its fruit how will you know when something grows along side of it that is not wheat? This is why Jesus said, *"you will know them by their fruit."* It's during the growing seasons that harvest becomes visible.

If someone claims to be seeking first the Kingdom of God, his or her life will exhibit righteousness. For example, if you are seeking first His Kingdom, you will not be seeking after materialistic things or have a love for money. If you are seeking first the Kingdom of God, you will not be living an immoral life, you will not be without love, you will not be unkind or harsh in your dealings with others. To put it in the most simplest of words, you cannot be living an ungodly life and be about the work of God! You cannot have one without the other. They are united beloved. They are inseparable.

Jesus knew that we would face not only difficulties in our lives as Christians during our stay here on this earth, but that we would also face false teachers. He wanted us to be warned that there will be those who come claiming to be followers of Christ but who are not. They will come doing great works seeming to be of God, but their hearts will be far from Him.

This brings us to our last principle for Kingdom Living.

Principle
Kingdom living is seeking God and His ways above all else

Before we can ever seek God's Kingdom and His righteousness we must stop seeking the things that we desire. We must stop seeking our way and abandon our way of thinking in order to embrace God's. What are some of the things that keep us from seeking God's Kingdom or His righteousness first?

_____

_____

_____

_____

_____

_____

Jesus said in **Matthew 16:24-27:**

"Then Jesus said to His disciples, 'If anyone wishes to come after Me, he must deny himself, and take up his cross and follow Me. For whoever

wishes to save his life will lose it, but whoever loses his life for My sake will find it. For what will it profit a man if he gains the whole world and forfeits his soul? Or what will a man give in exchange for his soul? For the Son of Man is going to come in the glory of His Father with His angels, and will then repay every man according to his deeds.'"

Self must be denied first before we can ever take up the cross of Calvary and the cross of Calvary must be taken up before we can ever begin to follow Jesus. At the very heart of Kingdom living is the heart that has denied its self; the heart that seeks after the Father.

When we seek God and His way above all else…

Benefit
Eternity will be the reward

What a reward we have waiting on us! Our future is so bright. This is how you know, beloved, that your reward is eternity.

John 14:1-3

"Do not let your heart be troubled; believe in God, believe also in Me. In My Father's house are many dwelling places; if it were not so, I would have told you; for I go to prepare a place for you. If I go and prepare a place for you, I will come again and receive you to Myself, that where I am, there you may be also."

These words have comforted me many times during my life and in the ministry the Lord has called me to. Seeking His Kingdom and His righteousness is a lifestyle, beloved. It is truly Kingdom Living. In this living there will be great difficulties, valleys to cross and wilderness journeys. There will be times when your soul becomes so dry and so thirsty that your Heavenly Father will bring forth water from the rock for you to drink. There will be times that the enemy will close in upon your life, surrounding you with fear and confusion leaving you no where to run. It is during those times that your Heavenly Father will bend low and, with His mighty hand He will part the mighty waters to lead you across to a safe place.

You will undoubtedly drink from the bitter waters along the way, but your Heavenly Father will take the bitterness of life and make it sweet. When the night is so dark, He will be a light unto your path so you will know the way in which you are to go. He will never leave you and He will never forsake you. He has a great work for you to do, beloved, and the reward is eternity with Jesus.

Let's review our Principles and Benefits from this week's lesson.

Principle # 1: *Kingdom living affects every aspect of our lives*
Benefit: *We will live for a higher purpose*

Principle # 2: *Kingdom living wears no mask*
Benefit: *Hypocrisy will vanish*

Principle #3: *Prayer is the lifeline of kingdom living*
Benefit: *The Kingdom of God is built*

Principle #4: *Kingdom living is seeking God and His ways above all else*
Benefit: *Eternity will be the reward*

How can we apply these truths to our lives?

Personal Evaluation

What are the priorities of your life?

What is the greatest desire of your heart?

How do you want to live out the rest of your days?

Where do you want to invest your time?

Are you a builder or are you a seeker? Are you either one?

Turn back to your chart on the blessed life. I know this has been a long week's study but this is so important. In looking at what Jesus tells us is the blessed life and remembering all that you have learned, how would you describe the blessed life now? Would you consider yourself to be a "blessed woman?" This is not a question I want you to write out your answer to, but rather spend time meditating over and talking with the Lord about. I understand the difficulty of this question. Would there be anything you would change about your pre-journey assignment answers now that you've taken this study?

It has been the delight of my heart to pilgrimage with you to the Sermon on the Mount. I pray that it has been a life-changing journey for you, my precious friend. May this generation rise up and call you "blessed!" Oh blessed woman of God, may you be the salt of the earth; that beautiful city set up on the hill for all to see and in the seeing, raise their eyes heavenward to praise the Heavenly Father. You have studied so hard, precious student and you have dug out some marvelous truths. What will you do with the truths that God has shown you? With knowledge comes accountability.

My prayer for you is that you will be like the wise man that Jesus spoke of in Matthew 7:24 and 25. It's these verses that I want to leave with you in the light of the truths that God has shown throughout the course of this study.

"Everyone who hears these words of Mine and acts on them, may be compared to a wise man who built his house on the rock. And the rain fell, and the floods came, and the winds blew and slammed against the house; and yet it did not fall, for it had been founded on the rock..."

May you be that wise woman! Much love to you, my precious friend and beloved student of God's Word. I have prayed for you and thanked God for allowing us the blessed privilege of opening up the Word of Life together. Though I may never see you face to face, know that I love you and am so very proud of you. Thank you for taking this course of study.

Pam Jenkins

Matthew 5:1-48

[1]When Jesus saw the crowds, He went up on the mountain; and after He sat down, His disciples came to Him.

[2]He opened His mouth and began to tech them, saying

[3]"Blessed are the poor in spirit, for theirs is the kingdom of heaven.

[4]"Blessed are those who mourn, for they shall be comforted.

[5]"Blessed are the gentle, for they shall inherit the earth.

[6]"Blessed are those who hunger and thirst for righteousness for they shall be satisfied.

[7]"Blessed are the merciful, for they shall receive mercy.

[8]"Blessed are the pure in heart, for they shall see God.

[9]"Blessed are the peacemakers, for they shall be called sons of god.

[10]"Blessed are those who have been persecuted for the sake of righteousness, for theirs is the kingdom of heaven.

[11]"Blessed are you when people insult you and persecute you, and falsely say all kinds of evil against you because of Me.

[12]"Rejoice and be glad, for your reward in heaven is great; for in the same way they persecuted the prophets who were before you.

[13]"You are the salt of the earth; but if the salt has become tasteless, how can it be made salty again? It is no longer good for anything, except to be thrown out and trampled under foot by men.

[14]"You are the light of the world. A city set on a hill cannot be hidden;

[15]"nor does anyone light a lamp and put it under a basket, but on the lampstand, and it gives light to all who are in the house.

[16]"Let your light shine before men in such a way that they may see your good works, and glorify your Father who is in heaven.

[17]"Do not think that I came to abolish the Law or the Prophets; I did not come to abolish but to fulfill.

[18]"For truly I say to you, until heaven and earth pass away not the smallest letter or stroke shall pass from the law until all is accomplished.

[19]"Whoever then annuls one of the least of these commandments, and teaches others to do the same, shall be called least in the kingdom of heaven; but whoever keeps and teaches them, he shall be called great in the kingdom of heaven.

[20]"For I say to you that unless your righteousness surpasses that of the scribes and Pharisees, you will not enter the kingdom of heaven.

²¹"You have heard that the ancients were told, 'YOU SHALL NOT COMMIT MURDER' and 'Whoever commits murder shall be liable to the court.'

²²"But I say to you that everyone who is angry with his brother shall be guilty before the court; and whoever says to his brother, 'you good-for-nothing,' shall be guilty before the supreme court; and whoever says, 'You fool,' shall be guilty enough to go into the fiery hell.

²³"Therefore if you are presenting your offering at the altar, and there remember that your brother has something against you,

²⁴"leave your offering there before the altar and go; first be reconciled to your brother, and then come and present your offering.

²⁵"Make friends quickly with your opponent at law while you are with him on the way, so that your opponent may not hand you over to the judge, and the judge to the officer, and you be thrown into prison.

²⁶"Truly I say to you, you will not come out of there until you have paid up the last cent.

²⁷"You have heard that it was said, 'YOU SHALL NOT COMMIT ADULTERY';

²⁸"But I say to you that everyone who looks at a woman with lust for her has already committed adultery with her in his heart.

²⁹"If your right eye makes you stumble, tear it out and throw it from you; for it is better for you to lose one of the parts of your body, than for your whole body to be thrown into hell.

³⁰"If your right hand makes you stumble, cut it off and throw it from you; for it is better for you to lose one of the parts of your body, than for your whole body to go into hell.

³¹"It was said, 'WHOEVER SENDS HIS WIFE AWAY, LET HIM GIVE HER A CERTIFICATE OF DIVORCE';

³²"but I say to you that everyone who divorces his wife, except for the reason of un-chastity, makes her commit adultery; and whoever marries a divorced woman commits adultery.

³³"Again, you have heard that the ancients were told, 'YOU SHALL NOT MAKE FLASE VOWS, BUT SHALL FULFILL YOUR VOWS TO THE LORD.'

³⁴"But I say to you, make no oath at all, either by heaven, for it is the throne of God,

³⁵" or by the earth, for it is the footstool of His feet, or by Jerusalem, for it is THE CITY FO THE GREAT KING.

³⁶"Nor shall you make an oath by your head, for you cannot make one hair white or black.

³⁷"But let your statement be, 'Yes, yes' or 'No, no'; anything beyond these is of evil.

³⁸"You have heard that it was said, 'AN EYE FOR AN EYE, AND A TOOTH FOR A TOOTH.'

³⁹"But I say to you, do not resist an evil person; but whoever slaps you on your right cheek, turn the other to him also.

⁴⁰"If anyone wants to sue you and take your shirt, let him have your coat also.

⁴¹"Whoever forces you to go one mile, go with him two.

⁴²"Give to him who asks of you, and do not turn away from him who wants to borrow from you.

⁴³"You have heard that it was said, "YOU SHALL LOVE YOU NEIGHBOR and hate your enemy.'

⁴⁴"But I say to you, love your enemies and pray for those who persecute you,

⁴⁵"so that you may be sons of your Father who is in heaven; for He causes His sun to rise on the evil and the good, and sends rain on the righteous and the unrighteous.

⁴⁶"For if you love those who love you, what reward do you have? Do not even the tax collectors do the same?

⁴⁷"If you greet only your brother, what more are you doing than others? Do not even the Gentiles do the same?

⁴⁸"Therefore you are to be perfect, as your heavenly Father is perfect."

Matthew 6:1-34

¹"Beware of practicing your righteousness before men to be noticed by them: otherwise you have no reward with your Father who is in heaven.

²"So when you give to the poor, do not sound a trumpet before you, as the hypocrites do in the synagogues and in the streets, so that you may be honored by men. Truly I say to you, they have their reward in full.

³"But when you give to the poor, do not let your left hand know what your right hand is doing,

⁴" so that your giving will be in secret; and your Father who ses what is done in secret will reward you.

⁵"When you pray, you are not to be like the hypocrites; for they love to stand and pray in the synagogues and on the street corners so that they may be seen by men. Truly I say to you, they have their reward in full.

⁶"But you, when you pray, go into your inner room, close your door and pray to our Father who is in secret, and your Father who sees what is done in secret will reward you.

⁷"And when you are praying, do no use meaningless repetition as the Gentiles do, for they suppose that they will be heard for their many words.

⁸"So do not be like them; for they your Father knows what you need before you ask Him.

⁹"Pray, then, in this way: 'Our Father who is in heaven, hallowed be Your name.

¹⁰'Kingdom come. Your will be done, on earth as it is in heaven.

¹¹'Give us this day our daily bread

¹²'And forgive us our debts, as we also have forgiven our debtors.

¹³'And do not lead us into temptation, but deliver us from evil. For Yours is the kingdom and the power and the glory forever. Amen.'

¹⁴"For if you forgive others for their transgressions, your heavenly Father will also forgive you.

¹⁵"But if you do not forgive others, then your Father will not forgive your transgressions.

¹⁶"Whenever you fast, do not put on a gloomy face as the hypocrites do, for they neglect their appearance so that they will be noticed by men when they are fasting. Truly I say to you, they have their reward in full.

¹⁷"But you, when you fast, anoint your head and wash your face

[18]" so that your fasting will not be noticed by men, but by your Father who is in secret; and your Father who sees what is done in secret will reward you.

[19]"Do not store up for yourselves treasures on earth, where moth and rust destroy, and where thieves break in and steal.

[20]"But store up for yourselves treasures in heaven, where neither moth nor rust destroys, and where thieves do not break in or steal;

[21]" for where your treasure is, there your heart will be also.

[22]"The eye is the lamp of the body; so then if your eye is clear, your whole body will be full of light.

[23]"But if your eye is bad, your whole body will be full of darkness. If then the light that is in you is darkness, how great is the darkness!

[24]"No one can serve two masters; for either he will hate the one and love the other, or he will be devoted to one and despise the other. You cannot serve God and wealth.

[25]"For this reason I say to you, do not be worried about your life, as to what you will eat or what you will drink; no for your body, as to what you will put on. Is not the life more than food, and the body more than clothing?

[26]"Look at the birds of the air, that they do not sow, no reap nor gather into barns, and yet your heavenly Father feeds them. Are you not worth much more than they?

[27]"And who of you by being worried can add a single hour to his life?

[28]"And why are you worried about clothing? Observe how the lilies of the field grow; they do not toil nor do they spin,

[29]" yet I say to you that not even Solomon in all his glory clothed himself like one of these.

[30]"But if God so clothes the grass of the field, which is alive today and tomorrow is thrown into the furnace, will he not much more clothe you? You of little faith!

[31]"Do not worry then, saying, 'What will we eat?' or 'What will we drink?' or 'What will we wear for clothing?'

[32]"For the Gentiles eagerly seek all these things; for your heavenly Father knows that you need all these things.

[33]"But seek first His kingdom and His righteousness and all these things will be added to you.

[34]"So do not worry about tomorrow; for tomorrow will care for itself. Each day has enough trouble of its own.

Matthew 7:1-29

[1]"Do not judge so that you will not be judged.

[2]"For in the way you judge, you will be judged; and by your standard of measure, it will be measured to you.

[3]"Why do you look at the speck that is in your brother's eye, but do not notice the log that is in your own eye?

[4]"Or how can you say to your brother, 'Let me take the speck out of your yes,' and behold, the log is in your own eye?

[5]"You hypocrite, first take the log out of your own eye, and then you will see clearly to take the speck out of your brother's eye.

[6]"Do not give what is holy to dogs, and do not throw your pearls before swine, or they will trample them under their feet, and turn and tear you to pieces.

[7]"Ask, and it will be given to you; seek, and you will find; knock, and it will be opened to you.

[8]"For everyone who asks receives, and he who seeks finds, and to him who knocks it will be opened.

[9]"Or what man is there among you who, when his son asks for a loaf, will give him a stone?

[10]"or if he asks for a fish, he will not give him a snake, willhe?

[11]"If you then, being evil, know how to give good gifts to your children, how much more will your Father who is in heaven give what is good to those who ask Him!

[12]"In everything, therefore, treat people the same way you want them to treat you, for this is the Law and the Prophets.

[13]"Enter through the narrow gate; for the gate is wide and the way is broad that leads to destruction, and there are many who enter through it.

[14]"For the gate is small and the way is narrow that leads to life, and there are few who find it.

[15]"Beware of the false prophets, who come to you in sheep's clothing, but inwardly are ravenous wolves.

[16]"You will know them by their fruits. Grapes are not gathered from thorn bushes nor figs from thistles, are they?

[17]"So every good tree bears good fruit, but the bad tree bears bad fruit.

[18]"A good tree cannot produce bad fruit, nor can a bad tree produce good fruit.

[19]"Every tree that does not bear good fruit is cut down and thrown into the fire.

[20]"So then, you will know them by their fruits.

[21]"Not everyone who says to Me, 'Lord, Lord,' will enter the kingdom of heaven, but he who does the will of My Father who is in heaven will enter.

[22]"Many will say to Me on that day, 'Lord, Lord, did we not prophesy in Your name, and in Your name cast out demons, and in Your name perform many miracles?'

[23]"And then I will declare to them, 'I never knew you; DEPART FROM ME, YOU WHO PRACTICE LAWLESSNESS.'

[24]"Therefore everyone who hears these words of Mine and acts on them, may be compared to a wise man who built his house on the rock.

[25]"And the rain fell, and the floods came, and the winds blew and slammed against that house; and yet it did not fall, for it had been founded on the rock.

[26]"Everyone who hears these words of Mine and does not act on them, will be like a foolish man who built his house on the sand.

[27]"The rain fell, and the floods came, and the winds blew and slammed against that house; and it fell and great was its fall."

[28]When Jesus had finished these words, the crowds were amazed at His teaching;

[29]for He was teaching them as one having authority and not as their scribes.

Word Windows

Blessed—*makarios*
It means happy, supremely blessed, well off.

City—(as used in Matthew 5:14) *polis*
A town enclosed with walls. A place where refuge is found. A community of the redeemed. It stands for inhabitants.

City—(old testament use) *ayar*
A place guarded by waking or a watch. In a wider sense it means an encampment or a post. It suggests a village.

Comforted—
To call near, to invite, invoke, consolation. It denotes to call to one's side or to call to one's aid.

Consider—*raah*
To see or look. To behold, respect or perceive. To provide, regard, to chose. To get acquainted with or to gain understanding of. It can mean to perceive or ascertain something without ever seeing it. It involves self examination or examination of a situation.

Create—*bara*
To create, to cut down, select. This verb only has God as its' subject. It demonstrates bringing an object or concept into being from previously non-existent material. To choose or make, done; make fat or dispatch—send out.

Filled—*chortazo*
To totter, to gorge. To supply in abundance. To be full, to satisfy completely even to overflowing.

Fret—*charah*
To glow or war, to blaze up, of anger, zeal or jealousy. It means wrath or hot or burning anger. To be earnestly displeased.

Gentle (KJV / Meek)—
Mildness of disposition, gentleness of spirit, meekness, humble.

Grace—*tachanuwn*
It is taken from the word: *chanan,* which means to stoop in kindness to an inferior; to favor, bestow, to implore. It means mercy, favor, to have pity upon.

Hallowed—*hagiazo*
To make holy, purify or consecrate. To set apart as holy.

Hunger—*peinao*
Toil or pine, famish, or crave. This word is akin to the Greek word: *penes*-which means to toil for daily subsistence. It means starving and can be translated poor. This word refers to one who is so poor that he earns his bread by daily labor. It means to work for one's daily bread.

Hypocrite—*hupokrite*
An actor underneath an assumed character. A stage player, a dissembler, deceit. It literally means one who wears a mask or behind the mask.

Inherit—*yaw-rash*
To occupy by driving out previous tenants and possessing in their place. It means to seize, to possess, to succeed or to drive out. It means; without fail or to subdue.

Know—*yada*
Observation, care or recognition; instruction, to understand or acknowledge. It means surety, familiar friend or kinsman. It means to know by observing or reflecting. It means to know through experience. This word can also represent the kind of knowing which one learns and can give back or impart to others. It implies opportunity to teach others about this kind of knowledge.

Light (new testament use)—*phos,* akin to *phao*
Face, to shine, or make manifest. In its widest application it means luminousness. To give light, expressing light as seen by the eye, to make to appear or evident. It means light-bearing.

Light (old testament use)—*owr*
Break of day, luminous, shine, fire, glorious, kindle. It is the opposition of darkness. NOTE: It is akin to the Hebrew word; *uwr*—which means; East the place where light comes from.

Love—*agapao*
Benevolence, or beloved. To love in a social or moral sense. It is a love that has no conditions. Is not self-seeking.

Maidservant—(kjv-handmaid)—*amah*
A female slave. A maid or bondwoman.

Meet—*yaad*
It means to fix upon by agreement or appointment. To direct or summon, to meet together, to assemble or set. It means to be betrothed.

Merciful—*eleemon*
To be actively compassionate. It means to pity but not just to be possessed of pity but actively extending it. It means to feel sympathy with the misery of another. It is sympathy manifested in act. It is the inward feeling of compassion which abides in the heart.

Mercy Seat—*hilasterion*
It means an expiatory (place or thing), an atoning victim, the lid of the ark, propitiation.

Mourn—*pentheo*
To grieve, to bewail primarily for the dead, but also includes any other passionate lamenting. A grief so all encompassing that it cannot be hidden. It means to lament or mourn over as a way of life.

Nabal—*nabal*
Stupid, wicked or foolish. It means a vile person. A person who is a fool.

Natural—*genesis*
Nativity. It's a birth, a begetting or producing.

Peace—*shalowm*
Safe, well, happy, prosperity. It means completeness or welfare. To be whole, tranquility, to be at ease.

Peacemaker—*eirenopoios*
Peaceable, to harmonize. It comes from the word: *"eirene"* which means prosperity, quietness or rest. To make peace.

Perfect—*teleios*
Complete, growth, character. Brought to an end, lacking nothing necessary for completeness, full grown. One who has attained the moral end for which he was intended.

Persecuted—*dioko*
To flee or pursue. To persecute. To follow after. To drive away.

Place—*tachath* taken from the same as *towach*
It means to depress, to humble. It means below or underneath. It means the bottom.

Poor—*ptochos*
Comes from the word "ptosso", which means to crouch. It means: beggar, pauper, poverty sticken, powerless to enrich or distressed. It means destitute.

Pray—*proseuchomai*
To supplicate, to worship. Comes from the root word *"pro"* which means; forward or toward. It means by the side of or nearness to.

Pure   *Katharos*
It means clean or clear. Free from impure admixture. Without blemish, spotless, free from corrupt desires. It refers to cleanness.

Refine—*tsaraph*
To fuse, to founder, to purge away, to casteth. It means to melt or to test, to find out who is qualified for battle. This word is equivalent to the English word for "Smith" as in Silver Smith.

Rend—*qara*
To tear or rend away. To cut or cut out. It is an expression of grief as when someone rends or tears their clothes.

Reproach—
To shame, disgrace, dishonor, to confound or put to blush.

Righteousness—*dikaiosune*
It is the character or quality of being right or just. It means equity of character, justification. It means straightness.

Salt—*halas*
It means prudence. It speaks of character and condition. It means to be possessed of purifying, perpetuating and antiseptic qualities. It is an emblem of the Covenant between God and His people. To stop corruption.

Seek—*zeteo*
To worship, to desire or to enquire. It means to go about or to strive after. It gives the sense of coveting earnestly. To demand or require. It means toward or to go about. To search for or to crave.

Thirst—*dipsao*
It means to thirst for literally or figuratively. It means to be athirst.

Tolerate—(KJV / sufferest)
To permit, to leave or let alone, to commit or suffer.

Willing (KJV / Free)—*nediybah*
Nobility or Reputation.

Worry—*(KJV / "take no thought")*—*merimnao*
To be anxious, to take care over. Distracting thought.

THE BLESSED LIFE

1. Blessed are: *They are poor in spirit*

2. Blessed are:

3. Blessed are:

4. Blessed are:

5. Blessed are:

6. Blessed are:

7. Blessed are:

8. Blessed are: